DISCARD

THE ARCHAEOLOGY OF NEW YORK

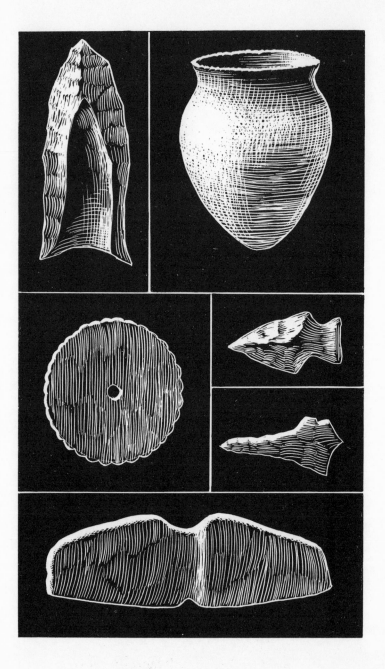

THE ARCHAEOLOGY OF
NEW YORK

BY ROBERT C. SUGGS

Illustrated by Leonard Everett Fisher

Thomas Y. Crowell Company · New York

BY THE AUTHOR

Modern Discoveries in Archaeology

The Archaeology of San Francisco

The Archaeology of New York

TO DONALD

CONTENTS

Introduction

SLOWLY AND SILENTLY the ship moved across the sparkling waters of the great bay. The September sun glinted on its brightly painted, salt-caked sides and illuminated the banners that flapped at mast-heads, bow, and stern. In the green bow, above the crimson-and-gold lion-figurehead, a sailor tossed and drew in the lead-weighted sounding line with a prac-ticed hand, shouting out the depth and the nature of the bottom. On the high poop deck, behind sky-blue railings painted with white cloud designs, the officers heard him, while they divided their attention be-tween the carefully reefed-in sails and the activities of the crew on deck, and scanned the shoreline for signs of life. The water was shallow in this bay and the wind, tricky: it would not be wise to hurry and come to grief on a sandbar after having crossed the whole Atlantic!

The ship glided closer and closer to the mouth of a great river that emptied into the bay, but the sound-ing line showed large shoals and dangerously shallow water across the mouth of the river. When the ship

1

had been eased into a sheltered spot with about thirty feet of water and a firm bottom, the leather-faced captain ordered the anchor dropped and the ship secured. The river could wait until it had been thoroughly scouted.

The tired crew looked out on the first land they had seen for weeks—a tranquil land of wooded, rolling hills, which sloped down to clean white sand beaches along the water's edge. In the water, schools of salmon and mullet glinted, and the batlike shadows of great rays occasionally swept to and fro. If the land was as rich in game as the sea was in fish, this new mysterious land would certainly be a marvelous place to settle.

The time was September 1609; the brilliantly painted little ship was the eighty-ton *Half Moon*, under the command of the English mariner, Henry Hudson; and the place was what is now known as Lower New York Bay. Although British by nationality, Hudson did not come in the name of the British king: the identity of his sponsors was proudly proclaimed from the masts of his little ship, where the flags of the city of Amsterdam, the seven provinces of the Netherlands, and the House of Orange flew in the breeze. The high stern, carved and painted with stars and a half-moon, bore the coat of arms of the city of Amsterdam and the words: *Vereenigde Oost*

Indische Compagnie—United East India Company. It was for this country that Hudson sailed, writing with his ship's wake another fascinating chapter in that most fascinating of periods of human history, the Age of Discovery.

This beautiful shoreline must indeed have seemed like a dream to the little crew, compared with their voyage up to that time. In search of a northeast passage to China, Hudson had driven his frail ship above the Arctic Circle into the icebergs and cruel winds of the Barents Sea. He had approached Novaya Zemlya, north of Russia, when the crew grew mutinous and he had to turn back. The crew chose to explore the coast of North America for a possible eastern passage to China, and so Hudson struck out across the Atlantic, stopping only at the bleak Faeroe Islands for water. An accident off Newfoundland forced a delay in the Kennebec River: then the *Half Moon* set sail again and struck the American coast somewhere around South Carolina, whence they "coasted" slowly north until they reached the site of what is today New York.

The arrival of the *Half Moon* had not gone unnoticed by the inhabitants of this new land, who were probably quite as excited as Hudson and his men. The *Half Moon's* progress up the bay to anchorage had surely been watched by many pairs of

3

dark brown eyes, set in bronze, wide-cheeked faces, peering from the safety of forest, bush, and rock.

On the day after arrival, Hudson moved the ship to a better anchorage and many Indians paddled out to the strange visitor who had come from so far beyond the edge of their world. Hudson's men distributed trinkets, knives, and beads to their feather-and-fur-clad visitors and took them on a grand tour of the ship. They saw the cannons, the crew's quarters, and the hold, but little seemed to capture the interest of the Indians so much as the large wooden block fastened to the deck by the mainmast, carved in the shape of a knight's head. Various rigging lines were passed through holes in this block, which was an important part of the ship's sailing apparatus. The Indians thought the image was a god and bowed down before it.

On the third day, Hudson sent out a boat crew, led by John Colman, to sound the entrance into the inner bay and the river mouth, known as "the Narrows" today. On their return, the sounding party was attacked by two canoes-full of Indians who volleyed arrows at them. Colman, an arrow through his neck, fell fatally wounded, while two other sailors received less serious wounds. Under the cover of darkness and a lucky rainsquall, the party returned to the *Half Moon* late the next morning. Colman was buried by the shore, the first known European casualty in a

long string of bitter fights between the Indians and
Europeans in the colony of New Netherland, as the
area would soon be called.

The entrance to the inner bay no longer a mystery,
Hudson entered the Narrows and moved up the bay
to the lower tip of Manhattan Island, where an Indian village stood. Although surrounded by canoes,
Hudson refused to allow the Indians aboard. He
feared treachery after the attack on Colman. Instead,
he traded with them for some fresh food, and, after a
few days, moved on up the river which now bears his
name.

And so European civilization came to Manhattan
Island, and the history of New York begins with the
arrival of the brave Henry Hudson. (To be sure,
Hudson was not the first European to enter the Narrows: the Italian navigator Giovanni da Verrazano
did so in 1524, sailing under the commission of
Francis I, King of France. Verrazano however only
stayed a short while. He did not go far into the inner
bay, and left only a sketchy account of his experiences. The Cabots may also have touched at New
York harbor on their voyages along the coast of
North America but we will never know, as their reports have been lost.) The discoveries of this deter-
mined British mariner opened the doors for a stream
of traders and settlers from Holland, soon after the
return of the *Half Moon* to home port. The beautiful

bay and the great river that emptied into it became an area of greatest interest for the Dutch and for other Europeans. Hudson's discovery was to change forever the lives of the Indian inhabitants of New Netherland. It would also change the future of the world, beyond Hudson's wildest dreams.

Today, New York is a sprawling, noisy city, its concrete and steel overflowing in all directions into the once quiet suburbs. It is a city of great complexity: great beauty and gross ugliness, wealth and terrible poverty, the old and the new, all side by side. The variety of scenes which greet an outsider as he goes from Harlem to Greenwich Village, from Central Park West to Fulton Street, from Wall Street to the "garment district," are too much to be absorbed. The streets are crowded with people of nearly every race and nationality in the world and one can hear many strange tongues spoken.

This city has played an enormous role in the history of our country. In a few short centuries it has been under Dutch, British, and American flags, and served for a time as the capital of the young United States. Enemy ships have often dropped anchor in its broad bay and, during the Revolution, great battles were fought in and around it. A crossroads of the world, it has welcomed floods of immigrants from all lands to help make the nation what it is today. It has also been the point of departure and return for American troops in many wars. The streets and sidewalks have felt the steps of many famous men and will feel the steps of many more to come.

But the history of New York as a city is only a short, last chapter in the long, long story of that great bay and its islands. More than ten thousand years *before* the appearance of the *Half Moon,* the woods and fields of the Manhattan area echoed to the sounds of human voices, speaking in languages long since lost to the ears of men. From Hudson's time on, the *history* of New York is to be found in the yellowed and dusty archives, diaries, letters, registries, and other documents that are the stock-in-trade of the historian. The *prehistory* of New York, however, must be sought in other places than libraries. It is in the earth below our feet, and its lengthy scroll can be read by archaeologists using scientific techniques.

This book, then, will describe the *prehistory* of the great city of New York as it has been reconstructed, bit by bit, through years of archaeological study. It is not a complete story, for time is like a great sieve: it only allows us to see a very small portion of what existed in the past. Languages, stories, chants and songs, names, and details of social organization all disappear before the onslaught of time. Objects of wood, leaves, and skin are extremely perishable; and, thus, only items of more durable material—stone, bone, shell—remain to be recovered by the archaeologist's trowel in most cases. Further, many archaeological sites are destroyed by natural causes or by man, and many are lost beneath rising tidelines or buried beneath layers of deposited earth.

The record of the archaeologist is never complete, and the archaeological record of New York is no exception. Nevertheless, what we do know presents a fascinating picture. From its beginning soon after the retreat of the last glacier, when mankind everywhere still hunted for food, the story of man in the New York area can be traced through many episodes that are important steps in human history—the disappearance of the great herds of migratory animals that lived in postglacial times; the introduction of corn, that magic plant of the American Indian; the introduction of pottery; and, finally, the arrival of the Europeans.

In some cases, no information is available from the New York area on a particular period in the past. In these cases, archaeological discoveries from nearby areas—New Jersey, the Hudson Valley, Connecticut —may give clues to what was going on in New York at that time.

The prehistory of New York is more than the reconstructed story of ancient life. It is also the story of the careful development and application of scientific methods and techniques that enable us, in this day of atomic weapons and space rockets, to open a small

window to look backward in time to those long vanished days. In this book, we will see how archaeologists excavate today, how they conducted their excavations in the past, and what differences the methods
make. We will also see how archaeologists analyze
what they have found and how they can tell what
their finds mean. Archaeologists are not the only individuals to whom credit must go in prehistoric studies, however, for geologists, geophysicists, ocean-
ographers, linguists, and historians have all made
contributions which will be mentioned.

The proper starting place of any story is at the
beginning, which calls for a very long step back in
time, to an era which is not clearly known, an era in
which the area that would someday be New York
looked very different. To begin at the beginning we
must go back to the end of the Pleistocene, or the Ice
Age.

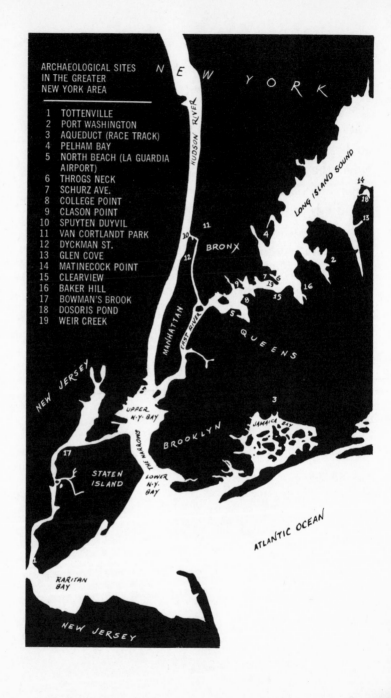

ARCHAEOLOGICAL SITES
IN THE GREATER
NEW YORK AREA

1 TOTTENVILLE
2 PORT WASHINGTON
3 AQUEDUCT (RACE TRACK)
4 PELHAM BAY
5 NORTH BEACH (LA GUARDIA
   AIRPORT)
6 THROGS NECK
7 SCHURZ AVE.
8 COLLEGE POINT
9 CLASON POINT
10 SPUYTEN DUYVIL
11 VAN CORTLANDT PARK
12 DYCKMAN ST.
13 GLEN COVE
14 MATINECOCK POINT
15 CLEARVIEW
16 BAKER HILL
17 BOWMAN'S BROOK
18 DOSORIS POND
19 WEIR CREEK

1 · Hunters of the Fluted Point

A LONG, flint-tipped spear balanced in his right hand, the old man moved through the thicket with the ease born of lifelong practice. His bright brown eyes, set deep in the wrinkled and weather-beaten face, seemed to look everywhere at once. The movement of a rabbit in the brush, the quick flight of a startled bird, the jagged cliffs across the valley, and the telltale marks of game on the forest floor were all seen and interpreted; yet he moved through the spruce and fir as silently as a wisp of smoke from a dying campfire, never touching the overhanging boughs, never losing his footing. Ahead of him, his two oldest sons, lean, hawk-faced, and also armed, moved with almost equal grace and speed as they broke trail and scouted ahead. Behind came the women, bent beneath the loads of food, clothing, equipment, and silent infants piled on their bent backs. The youngest son, yet without a wife, brought up the rear, carefully leaving blazes and signs for the other families, far behind them, to see.

The wind whipped through the trees and the old

man felt its bite slightly through his fur jacket and skin trousers. Soon the snow would fall, but by then they would be far to the south, where winter's sting did not cut so deep and the game was more plentiful.

For many days they had pushed southward over the rolling foothills along the east flank of the valley. In the broad valley floor on both sides of the river they could always see the dark masses of bison and the occasional towering bulk of a herd of mastodon. The sky overhead was sometimes crossed by V's and long sinuous lines of migratory fowl, also fleeing the cold of winter.

This was the way life was; this was the way it had always been as far as the old man knew, or as far back as any legends of his people went. South in the winter, north in the summer, always in pursuit of the life-giving game: the hairy, tusked mastodon; the hump-backed, snorting bison; and the proud caribou.

Where the herds moved, they followed to pick off the stragglers and strays, camping on the sites of their kills, and then moving on. The trees, bushes, and plants of the vast woodland provided nuts, berries, and roots and the streams were alive with fish.

Soon they would be at the Place Where the Rivers Meet, the old man thought. His eyes greeted as old friends every landmark, learned from his more than forty winters on this trail. They would come down onto a broad plain, rimmed with hills. Rivers flowed onto this plain from east and west to join the Great River and course together out to the sea through a break in the hills. There the hunting was good, for the animals could not always ford the rivers and would trap themselves. There, too, they would meet other bands of men—those who hunted over by the sea to the east.

He thought of his sister, bent and worn now, who years ago had moved to the camp of one of the hunters there. His younger brother, Black Bear, had also taken his spears and moved eastward in search of better hunting on the northward trek many summers before. It would be fine to see them and trade tales. The other families following the old man and his sons would catch up and there would be a great reunion. They would hunt together, make a big kill among the animals trapped in the river junctions, and then have a feast. Then they would cross the great river, head out onto the plain by the sea, and move south quickly.

A low whistle came from ahead. The old man froze in his tracks and looked to see the eldest son's signal through the thicket. He moved swiftly to join him and saw below a little group moving out of a side valley. The old man strained his eyes. Not all men were friendly. Yes, they were friends! He could recognize Black Bear's waddle anywhere, even after so many years. "Go, meet them," he told the boy. "I'll get the others. But wait: be careful of Black Bear's son-in-law. He is nervous, and his spear flies quickly." The old man smiled and hummed a hunting chant as he hurried to collect the well-hidden women and the boy. He could almost smell the bison chunks over the campfire and hear the dancers' feet beat out the time as they danced through the firelight. The weight of forty-five winters was no longer so heavy. This was a good life!

This incident might well have occurred in the life of an inhabitant of New York State some eleven thousand years or so ago, as he journeyed down the Hudson to what is now the site of New York City. The inhabitants of the Americas of that time are known to archaeologists as the Paleo-Indians (Old Indians) to distinguish them from all later archaeological Indian cultures. The Paleo-Indians were the first groups, so far as is now known, to inhabit the vastness of the North and South American continents. They came, or their ancestors came, from eastern Asia sometime during the period when the last glacier had spread its groaning, grinding bulk across the northern portion of North America, at a time perhaps as long ago as fifteen thousand years (some scientists have suggested forty thousand!).

There are no known traces of Paleo-Indian inhab-

16

itants in the metropolitan New York area, but there are very good reasons for this which will be mentioned later. To reconstruct life in that area so long ago, we will have to depend on information gathered from archaeological and geological investigations in other parts of New York State, Pennsylvania, Connecticut, and Massachusetts, and also use general knowledge of the way of life of the Paleo-Indians throughout the whole United States east of the Rockies.

The New York that the Paleo-Indians may have camped in was a very different place in that far-off time. The glacier was still not many hundreds of miles to the north and the cold air blowing from its bulk influenced the climate considerably. The land was covered with forests of spruce and fir; bogs, ponds, and streams were numerous in the summer. The glaciers had drawn up so much seawater from the oceans of the world that sea level was considerably lower than at present.

Geophysicists and climatologists have probed deep into bogs and lagoon bottoms along the Massachusetts, Connecticut, New Jersey, and Virginia coasts to determine just how far the sea level did drop. The story of this process is written in ancient deposits of peat (partly carbonized and decomposed vegetable matter, especially mosses) now buried deep beneath the present shorelines. Peat of certain kinds is formed along shorelines: this is the kind the geophysicists search for, using a hollow borer or soil-auger to penetrate forty-five feet or more beneath the surface. The peat brought up in these borings can be dated by the carbon-14 dating method and the history of sea-level changes traced in this fashion.

It appears that the sea level around New York in Paleo-Indian time may have been nearly one hundred feet below the present level and certainly was more than fifty feet lower! What a difference this drop in sea level made! Long Island Sound must have been a large flat plain with a small arm of the sea traversing it. The coast would have been located miles beyond the Narrows, and New York Bay would have been a basin, in which the Hudson was joined by a number of smaller streams. The Hudson mouth itself was certainly much narrower in that time.

Stranger than the landscape of Paleo-Indian time were the animals that roamed it. Mastodons, those creatures of modern science-fiction and comic strips, were very real inhabitants of New York then. They ranged the hills and valleys, grazing and browsing on the vegetation that sprang from the recently glaciated soil. Their skeletons, or parts of skeletons, have been found in many places in New York State. One of the most famous finds occurred in Cohoes, not far from Troy. The remains of some of the mastodons have been dated by the carbon-14 technique. A mastodon found at Kings Ferry, N.Y., was dated at 11,410 ± 410 years ago; another, at Sheridan, N.Y., at 9,200 ± 500 years ago. In Sussex County, N.J., still another mastodon was dated at 10,896 ± 200 years ago.

And the mastodons were not the only game hunted by the Paleo-Indians, for with the mastodons traveled herds of bison and caribou, as well as the numerous other animals of the subarctic woodlands. The mastodons appear to have become extinct by eight thousand years ago. The bison, however, survived in a much changed form into early colonial times in western New York State.

Hunters of the Fluted Point

The Paleo-Indians, themselves, were hunters of a kind that was found throughout most of Europe, Asia, and northern Africa at that time. They preyed on the great herds of migratory animals that lived in the postglacial world, following them about on their yearly movements. Archaeologists have found no Paleo-Indian sites that show evidence of long habitation. Most, in fact, seem to have been camps inhabited for a few days only, at or near the place where a large animal had been killed. When the fresh meat was exhausted, the hunters would move on, leaving the dismembered carcass, a few stone chips, some broken tools, and a spearpoint or so around the ashes of their campfires. These sites are few and isolated: most Paleo-Indian finds are single spearpoints, picked up on the surface of the ground where they have been washed out by rain or uncovered by farming.

From these facts, archaeologists have concluded that the Paleo-Indian population of North America was very small and thinly spread over the vast continent. By plotting the finds of Paleo-Indian points on maps, archaeologists have found that these early settlers may have been concentrated in the valleys of the Ohio, Tennessee, and upper Mississippi Rivers. In fact, it is likely that their preferred routes of travel were in or along the great river valleys or the coastal plains. Movement would have been much easier in such terrain than in mountains, for example, and the game on which life depended would also have stuck to the valleys. The site of today's New York City, at the junction of a large river valley and a wide coastal plain, must have been visited many times by these long-dead hunters.

It is not only the small size of the Paleo-Indian population that makes their traces so hard to find. Tremendous changes in the surface of the earth have destroyed or hidden many of those traces forever. In the New York City area, for example, the rising sea may have buried remains of Paleo-Indian camps beneath tons of mud, silt, and water. The action of wind and rain may have washed away other sites and mixed up stone tools, animal bones, and charcoal from campfires with tons of gravel and earth in valleys. Man, the destroyer, has also played a large part in eliminating the traces of his predecessors on the

21

land. With so much building on and around Manhattan Island it is a wonder that any Indian artifacts have survived at all, not to mention scarce Paleo-Indian artifacts.

The mark of these ancient hunters is a long, narrow spearpoint with a deep groove or "flute" down each side: a spearpoint that is as easily recognizable to an archaeologist as a bison track was to a Paleo-Indian. These points are made of flint, chert, or other stones composed of silica. The Paleo-Indians' spears were obviously meant for heavy duty: the points average about three inches in length, but are sometimes as large as five inches. The entire point was chipped out and shaped by the Indian craftsman, first with hammerstones for rough shaping and then with antler flakers to pry loose small flakes. Then flutes or grooves, which ran from the base of the point toward the tip, were made. Several flakes were removed from each side to make the grooves. This must have been a touchy operation, even for the skilled Paleo-Indian hunters. Many points were probably shattered at this stage by a misdirected blow with a hammerstone. Nevertheless, the finished spearpoints stand as some of the finest examples of American Indian industry, with a rugged beauty all their own.

The purpose of the grooves or flutes is not clear. They may have made it easier to fasten the heavy point to a split spear shaft. On the other hand, they may have acted as "blood-gutters," such as one sees on a modern infantryman's bayonet, to permit the blood to flow from the wound with the point in place.

Fluted points are also called Clovis points by archaeologists, after the town near which they were first found: Clovis, New Mexico. They have not been discovered anywhere *very* close to New York City, but the finds nevertheless seem to indicate what we have suspected to be true: that Paleo-Indians were frequent visitors to what would some-day be Manhattan Island. Along the Hudson River, from Saratoga County right down to Orange County, fluted points have given evidence of bands moving up and down the valley. Mr. Frank Glynn, a dedi-cated amateur archaeologist from Clinton, Connect-icut, found a fluted point on the shore of Long Island Sound. Another large fluted point was turned up in East Hartford, Connecticut, by an "Indian relic" col-lector many years ago and is now in the American Museum of Natural History. Paleo-Indians also scat-tered their points throughout New Jersey, and in Pennsylvania, one of the biggest Paleo-Indian sites in the East is on a farm not far from Harrisburg, where several hundred artifacts have been found. Archaeologists have come across fluted points all over Pennsylvania, mainly in stream valleys. Massa-chusetts also was visited by the far-ranging hunters, for over one hundred fluted points and three thousand other Paleo-Indian artifacts have been located at a place called Bull Brook, near Ipswich, Massachusetts. Thus, New York City is surrounded by Paleo-Indian finds, and it is hard to believe that those early settlers of America did not pass by the site of the city many, many times, as they hunted up and down the river valleys and the coastal plains.

The few Paleo-Indian sites that are relatively large have enabled archaeologists to determine that these hunters did, in fact, live at the same time as the now-extinct bisons and mastodons. To begin with, Clovis points are found *in the skeletons* of such animals. Then, campfires on Clovis sites have been dated by the carbon-14 method and nearly all fall between the dates of 11,500 and 11,000 years ago. In some parts of the country, including the eastern states, Clovis hunters may have stayed on until 9,000 years ago, however. (None of the sites very near New York has been dated by the carbon-14 method. Dates of 9,300 ± 400 years and 6,940 ± 800 years were obtained at the Bull Brook site, which is the nearest dated site to New York.)

What else does archaeology tell about the way of life of the Paleo-Indian? That he made use of extensive quantities of animal skins is shown by the numerous stone skin scrapers found on most sites of any size. These scrapers were made of flakes of flint or

24

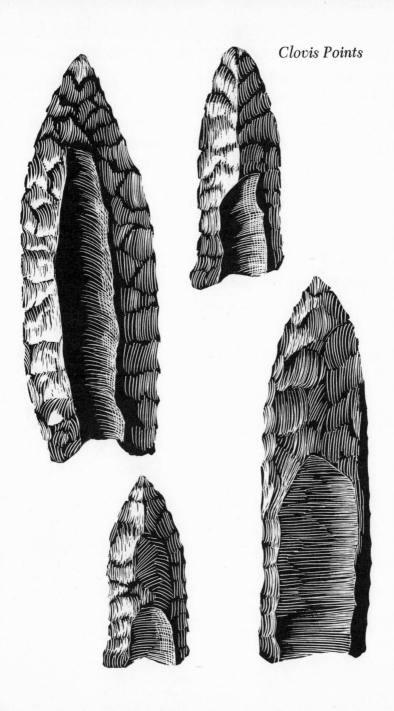

Clovis Points

chert. The edges and ends of the flakes were chipped to give a thick flat surface with sharp corners, which was used to scrape fat and muscle tissue in preparing skins. The skins so prepared were probably fashioned into some kind of clothing. No bone needles or awls such as could be used for making skin clothing have been found in the eastern United States but they have been found in Clovis point sites in the western states.

Along with the stone scrapers are found flake knives—stone flakes on which sharp edges have been produced by carefully removing small flakes along one or both sides of an edge. Small stone drills and gravers—flakes with sharp, needlelike projections used for engraving or fine carving—also were in the Paleo-Indian tool kit. The knives could have been used in skinning and butchering, as well as in woodworking or to produce the spearshafts, knife handles, and other wooden utensils of the hunters. Some of the stone scrapers described above might also have been used for that purpose.

The houses of the Paleo-Indians are a mystery as yet. They probably made flimsy brush structures like windbreaks or lean-tos, lived in rock shelters or caves, or simply lived in the open during better weather. At any rate, no traces of any forms of houses have as yet been found.

At some time around 8000 B.C., the world of the

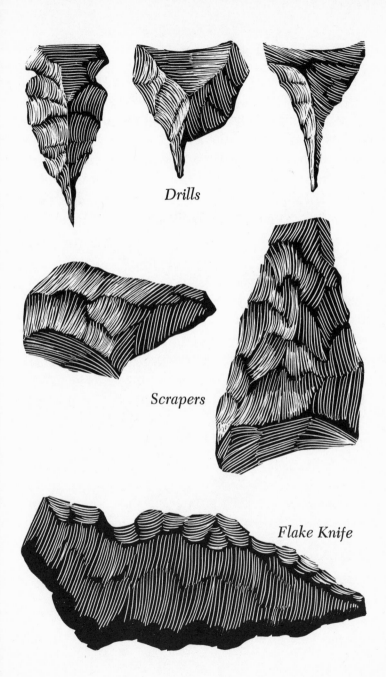

Drills

Scrapers

Flake Knife

Paleo-Indian began to change. The climate was becoming warmer and the sea level rising. The firs and spruce were disappearing gradually and giving way to forests of pine, oak, and other leafy trees. The herds of bison and mastodon were beginning to get smaller and disappear, possibly as a result of Indian marksmanship, possibly because of the changing environment. Other, more familiar, animals inhabited the forests in larger numbers—bear, deer, fox, elk, wolf, and others. The old migratory hunting life drew quietly and slowly, ever so slowly, to a close over a period of many centuries. The way of the Paleo-Indian was no more. The long sharp fluted points no longer sang through the air, thirsting for mastodon blood. The first of many great changes had come over the Indian inhabitants of New York. When next we pick up the faint trail of prehistoric New Yorkers, life and the world will have changed a good deal.

2 · Stone Workers of the Forests

THE WIND SHRIEKED through the frozen whiteness of the forest and stripped weak, brittle branches from the naked oaks. The snow-laden pines tossed and bent, giving off clouds of powdery snow that bit into the face like tiny icicles. Bundled in hooded fur jackets, fur trousers, and mittens, their feet wrapped in layers of soft skins, the two men stood, shielding their eyes against the blast of icy needles. They looked intently at the rocky hillside a few hundred feet away. There, beneath a slab of gray frosted rock, the dark entrance to a small cave could be seen, almost blocked by a snowdrift. As quietly as possible, the two men moved across the crusted snow toward the opening. The elder remembered the cave from a summer day many summers back when he had passed that way. It was not very big, but *maybe big enough for a bear*. Perhaps they would have good luck!

The winter had been vicious and game had been scarce, driven away by the cold or, perhaps, by the

Animal Spirits, angry because the hunters had not
performed their hunting magic faithfully. Pangs of
hunger had forced the brothers out into the bleak
landscape from the shelter of their own winter cave
to search for food for themselves and the women and
children who starved in wide-eyed silence. The supply of acorns, dried berries, dried meat, and smoked
fish and shellfish that they had put aside months before, when winter was only a tingle in the air and a
few turning leaves, needed to be stretched out.

It was a far cry from the warm summer days by the
sparkling seashore, when they had fished and collected shellfish to bring home to the domed thatch-
roof lodge in which they lived during that season.

They cautiously approached the cave mouth, carefully drawing down their face wrappings to sniff the
air within. The rank smell of a hibernating bear hit
two pairs of dilated nostrils hard. The brothers
exchanged grins; they backed away a few paces to
plan the attack, their mittened hands tense around
their long spears and spear-throwers.

"The cave is small and tight," said the elder; "it
curves like a dog's leg. The bear is probably all the
way in and we will have to get him outside to kill
him."

"There is no room for a hard thrust in there?"
asked the younger.

"No," came the grim reply, "we must wound him

in the cave. Listen: I'll crawl in, and you climb up on the rock over the entrance. If I can, I'll spear him, and get out fast. He'll be right behind me. When he hits the snowdrift he'll flounder in it and be blinded for a moment. Then you drive your point in at the base of his skull or into his ribs. We'll finish him off with the axes."

The eyes of the younger were wide with surprise at this bold plan. He had learned long ago, however, to do as his brother directed without asking questions. He took up his position over the top of the cave entrance while his brother cleared away the snow and, stooping low, entered the dark hole.

As his brother's legs disappeared below him, the younger man drew forth a curious pear-shaped stone object from a pouch in the depths of his furs and stroked it briefly, muttering a prayer to the spirit of this ancient stone.

Inside the cave, the elder paused to let his eyes adjust to the darkness and breathed a magical charm. The time went by slowly, but gradually he could make out more and more of the shape of the walls and floor and he slowly moved in, swimming in the scent of the sleeping bear. A rustling sound came from within, and the intruder paused, hoping that the bear was not a light sleeper. When he had rounded the dogleg turn, he could see into the blackness where the animal slept. It was possible to make

33

out a formless dark shadow in the gloom, but he could not tell which end was head and which tail. The passage was tighter than he thought; his bulky clothes hampered his movements. He raised his arm and cautiously moved the spear around to gauge how much clear space he had. He would have to throw from an awkward position, his arm less than half drawn back. Carefully he poised for the thrust and sent it home, then began a scuffling hands-and-knees retreat as the cave erupted with a great roar and shrieks of pain. In the wider entrance, he turned around and broke out of the door to the right. The bear was not far behind. Its jaws were bloody and blood welled from around the broken spear shaft in its side.

On the roof of the cave the younger brother balanced on his toes, his spear notched into his spear thrower, its broad flat point aimed toward the spot where the animal should appear. The furious bruin burst out into the snowdrift in a cloud of snow and blood and stumbled. His long neck was stretched out for a split second. In that instant the boy threw his spear with every ounce of strength he could muster at the hackles that bristled over the base of the flat skull. The spear went straight to its mark and he leaped after the shaft to grab it and drive it deeper. The elder ran up, clutching a short-handled stone axe with a hard keen edge—

34

In a few minutes it was over. The bear was rather large and still had a sizable amount of fat under his matted brown fur. The fatty meat and the grease would provide them with nourishment for many days to come, the teeth with a necklace or some carving tools, and the skin would make a good sleeping robe. "And the magic: we will not forget the magic," thought the elder as they dragged the carcass home. He was already thinking of how he would make a special altar on which to place the skull to help appease the Bear Spirit who watched over all bears to see that hunters who killed them were respectful.

The world of the Paleo-Indian and his way of life disappeared from the prehistoric record. Somewhere in the vast woodlands of eastern North America a new way of life developed, a way of life better adapted to the changed environment. It is not certain if the new way of life was developed by the Paleo-Indians themselves over a period of centuries or perhaps even thousands of years. Some archaeological evidence suggests that this is so: Paleo-Indian points have been found around sites of this new culture. On the other hand, the new way of life may have been brought into the new world by fresh immigrants from Asia.

As the imaginary incident at the start of the chapter indicates, the new way of life was characterized by the hunting of small game in forests much like those of today. Food was more plentiful. The people lived a much more settled life than their Paleo-Indian predecessors. This new way of life lasted for a period of approximately three thousand years in New York State and the surrounding region, a period called the Archaic ("Old") period. The way of life, or the remains that archaeologists find of it, is known as the Archaic culture.

The Archaic period is well represented in the New York metropolitan area. The Grantville site, situated on College Point across from La Guardia Airport, held a very rich collection of Archaic spearpoints, scrapers, axes, and assorted stone tools. The Dyckman Street site was situated at the foot of Dyckman Street. Here a large Indian midden or trash disposal heap contained artifacts of the Archaic in the lower levels, followed by more recent artifacts on top. Two sites, less well known, were found along Weir Creek and Schurz Avenue on Throgs Neck. These also contained artifacts from later times as well as those of the Archaic period. Just outside the metropolitan area an Archaic site has been found at Glen Cove, Long Island. Several excellent Archaic sites lie further east on the island, as well as up the Hudson River, at such places as Croton Point and Bannerman's Island.

Before examining the Archaic period further,

there are two points that should be borne in mind. The Archaic period lasted for three thousand years or more: during that immense time, many minor changes took place in the Archaic way of life. New tools were invented, old ones discarded; better ways of doing things were found. Trade from other parts of North America brought in new ideas and objects, and new groups of people may have migrated in. In addition to the changes that occurred through time during the Archaic period, we know that there were differences between groups of Archaic hunters living at the same time, only a few miles from each other. And so when we may speak of early and later Archaic tools, or Archaic people of northern New York or eastern Long Island, we are speaking of the variations in the basic Archaic culture that the archaeologist has been able to recognize in time as well as space.

The world of the Archaic hunters was a much pleasanter world than that of the Paleo-Indians. The Archaic culture existed during what geologists call the "climatic optimum": a long period of good climate following the coldness of the Ice Age. The climate had warmed considerably and was probably much the same as today. The great glacial ice sheet had melted under the increased warmth and given back to the seas a great deal of the seawater it had taken away. In addition, the whole surface of the land along the East Coast was sinking in places (and still is!), due to very slow, but powerful, movements of great sections of the earth's crust and core. By 5000 B.C. or so, the sea level was approximately where it is today. Further climate changes, between 5000 B.C. and the time of Christ, caused the level of the sea to fluctuate, rising as much as ten feet above or sinking ten feet below the present level. Every period of high sea level was related to a period of warmer weather, while the drops in sea level were related to cooler periods. These periods were not short: they were centuries in length, and the total change in average temperature might have been no more than four or five degrees Fahrenheit from cold to warm periods.

The trees and vegetation among which the Archaic people lived were much the same as those found by the colonists when they arrived here. Oak, maple, pine, hemlock, hickory, and beech trees made up the forests that covered the hills and valleys in a green cloak. Along the forest floor ran deer, elk, bear, fox, and wolf. Woodchucks burrowed in the thick dark soil beneath the towering trees which were alive with squirrels, and beavers labored in the streams with their engineering construction work.

The Archaic people of prehistoric New York seemed to have lived at least part of the year on the shore of Long Island Sound or along the rivers where they could gather shellfish and fish. The sites in the New York metropolitan area are all of this shore type. They were probably inhabited during the warmer seasons. There is evidence from other parts of the East Coast that during the winter the Archaic people may have gone inland in smaller groups. These Archaic sites are characterized by *middens*: deposits of discarded sea or freshwater shells, in which are mixed animal bones, artifacts, charcoal, and dark earth stained by decomposing vegetable and animal matter discarded by the hunters. Fire pits or hearths are sometimes found, as are pits filled with midden material.

No traces of Archaic houses have been found in

the metropolitan area, although on the site in Glen Cove, called the Garvie's Point site, a rectangular cleared area that might have been a house floor was found, surrounded by a low wall of stones. In Massachusetts, entire Archaic houses with circular floor plans have been excavated, while house floors of uncertain shape have been found in upper New York. It is likely that the houses which stood on the New York sites were circular or oval, made of a framework of branches covered with thatch or bark.

Hunting provided a good portion of the food consumed by the Archaic people, and also accounted for the production of many of the stone artifacts through which archaeologists have learned of the Archaic life. Many kinds of stone projectile points are found on the Archaic sites of New York City. Early Archaic projectile points are long and narrow, with small notches in the sides of the base for the fine wrappings of thong or fiber with which the point was attached to the shaft. In later Archaic times the points were shorter and much broader, triangular in shape, with small side notches. Long points with narrow stems were also used. Many of the points of the Archaic New Yorkers were made of quartz. This mineral does not flake or chip well and is very hard. Other points were made of flint, slate, and a stone called argillite found in New Jersey. From the size of the points, it appears that most if not all were intended to be used on spears. It is not certain whether the bow and arrow was known to the Archaic Indians of the New York area.

The Archaic men probably made their own spearpoints, for the most part, although they seem to have obtained stone to make points or perhaps finished arrowpoints from other groups by trade. Making pro-

jectile points must have been a difficult, tedious job, calling for lots of skill and patience. The hunter had only stones to use as hammers—many have been found with ends battered from hammering on other stones. With the hammerstones, the "roughing-out" of the point could be done. Then a piece of strong antler would be used for finer "pressure flaking," to shape the point correctly and make sure it was very sharp. In pressure flaking small chips are removed from the edges of a piece by pressing forcefully with a hard tool.

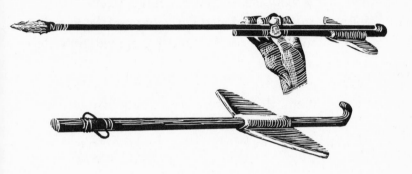

Spear throwers were also in use, equipped with elaborately fashioned stone weights. The spear thrower is a very handy device that works like a lever, giving added force to the spear when thrown. It is a stick or narrow board fitted with a hand grip near one end and a hook or groove to catch the butt of the spear at the other end.

The hunter placed the spear on the spear thrower, holding it in place on the board with the fingers of his throwing hand, which curled around both spear and spear thrower. The spear thrower projected out between his thumb and forefinger. In effect it lengthened his arm by a foot or more, and multiplied the power with which the spear could be propelled at the target.

Stone Workers of the Forests

One of the most curious artifacts of the Archaic is the stone spear-thrower weight, or "bannerstone." The name *bannerstone* comes from a time, not too long ago, when archaeologists did not know what these stone objects were, and concluded that they were used as decorations on scepters or ceremonial staffs by important people in the Archaic settlements. Thus, they were called "bannerstones." Archaeologists have a weakness for classifying as ceremonial objects any artifacts that they can't classify any other way (often they're right!).

The bannerstones used by the Archaic hunters of New York are generally made of steatite or other soft stone, and shaped like an airplane wing, three to four inches long. They were attached to the spear thrower by a hole drilled laboriously right through the center of the wing, or were tied on by cords passed through notches on the bannerstone.

The holes in the stones were probably made with wooden drills, using quantities of sand for abrasive, and even greater quantities of patience. The external shape of the bannerstone was produced by chipping away the stone until a rough outline was obtained, then pecking with a sharp hard stone at the rough spots to wear them down, and finally polishing with sand and water or skin.

When fitted on the spear thrower, the weight of the bannerstone would act to increase even further the

46

force with which the spear could be thrown. Many of these bannerstones, particularly in the later Archaic period, are carefully polished, far beyond what was required for a simple stone weight. In addition to their use as weights on spear throwers, these very attractive objects could still have been insignia of tribal rank among the Archaic people.

Hunting not only provided meat, but a great number of other raw materials used in different ways. Skins were a very important item for clothing, bedding, and thongs. The skins, of course, have long disappeared, but the stone scrapers with which the skins were carefully scraped (probably by Archaic women), so long ago, are still found in Archaic sites. Several different varieties were found at Grantville. Another interesting and unusual stone implement of the Archaic period is the semilunar knife, or *ulu* (the Eskimo word for a similar tool used until very recently). These artifacts are semicircular in shape, the flat edge left thick, and the rounded edge chipped and ground to a cutting edge. In late Archaic sites they were highly polished, and are beautiful specimens of Indian craftsmanship. One such *ulu* was found at the Schurz Avenue site on Throgs Neck, while an unpolished one was found at the Grantville site.

To sew the skins of the animals into garments, the bones of the very same animals were used for awls to

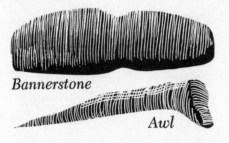

Bannerstone

Awl

Ulu

punch holes in skins and for needles. Some small decorated bone objects have been found that may be ornaments. In western New York, an early Archaic culture called the Lamoka culture was characterized by large quantities of worked bone: awls, needles, spearpoints, hairpins, etc. Their cousins on prehistoric Manhattan did not appear to use as much bone however.

In the warmer seasons, fishing and shellfishing probably took up the time of the men. The clam and oyster beds around the metropolitan area must have been huge in those days and the supply probably seemed limitless to the Indians. They certainly left enough empty shells on their abandoned campsites. Today, of course, years of industrial pollution have banished edible shellfish from the whole metropolitan area, and it is not possible to tell just where and how large the prehistoric shellbeds were.

Fishing appears to have been done mainly with nets, although hooks made of a perishable substance like wood may have been used. Although no Archaic

Stone Workers of the Forests

Needle

Spearpoint

Netsinker

nets have survived the long years, the stone netsinkers—oval or round stones with notches for lashing—remain to tell the tale. In upper New York State one site produced 6,000 netsinkers, indicating that the Archaic men of that locality must really have done a great deal of fishing! It is certain that the Archaic people of prehistoric New York spread their nets in the coastal shallows, bays, and river mouths.

In addition to nets, *weirs*, or fish traps made of sticks and stones, were probably used to catch fish with the rise and fall of the tide. We can assume that these people were also quite capable of making canoes, probably dugouts, from which they could conduct their fishing in the deeper waters. Using nets of any size at all in fishing operations pretty much requires the use of boats. Furthermore, the Archaic people crossed water barriers like the Hudson and Long Island Sound, which would have been very difficult without boats.

The wealth of the forest was undoubtedly put to great use by the Archaic people, who must have

49

relied heavily on nuts, berries, roots, and leaves of various kinds, as primitive peoples all over the world still do to this day. Cylindrical stone pestles for crushing and grinding plant foods have been found in the Grantville and Throgs Neck sites, but no mortars have turned up as yet. It seems likely that the New York City Archaic people probably used wooden mortars to prepare their plant foods. Smaller grinding implements, called "mullers," have been found in coastal Archaic sites outside the New York area. These were used with small stone slabs.

The Archaic tool kit for woodworking was by no means poor. Stone adzes and axes were made for use in woodworking, and probably in warfare and hunting as well. An adze is a tool with its cutting edge at right angles to the axis of the handle, like a hoe. Such a tool is particularly useful for shaping the inside surfaces of canoes and bowls. Stone axe blades (their cutting edges parallel to the long axis of handle) were of two types: a smaller kind with smooth surfaces that was fitted into a socket in the wooden handle and wedged or glued there, and an axe blade which was encircled with a deep groove so that it could be fitted into a split wooden handle.

The religions of the American Indian are very interesting subjects of study, full of colorful tales of strange gods and heroes in fabulous times in the past. Unfortunately, these marvelous tales do not survive

Axe Blade

Plummet Stone

in archaeological sites. Very little has survived in the New York metropolitan area to tell us about the religion of the Archaic inhabitants there. We have the so-called "plummet stones" (one of which was found at Grantville), which are thought to be magical charms of some type or other. They simply do not seem to have had any other conceivable use. No burials have been found in the metropolitan area to tell us anything about the views that the Archaic people might have had of the afterlife. In other areas, not too far from New York City, the Archaic graves show evidence of some strange burial customs. In Massachusetts, for example, at the Wapanucket site, Archaic graves contained ashes of cremated human bodies. On eastern Long Island, a cemetery of the late Archaic at Orient Point also contained cremations in large pits, with ceremonial fires nearby, and large quantities of points, axes, ornaments, and utensils of various types, some of which had been broken purposely before being placed in the grave.

The Archaic period, as we know it today, is the result of lots of work by archaeologists in very recent years. In the 1920's, two archaeologists working in New York State, Dr. Alanson Skinner and Dr. Arthur C. Parker, used the word *archaic* to refer to what they thought were the oldest Indian artifacts, such as pottery and arrowpoints, then in their collections. It seems that they had decided that the artifacts that looked crude or clumsy were the oldest, while those that looked more refined were more recent. They did not always make use of the *stratigraphic* excavation techniques used by modern archaeologists. The stratigraphy of an archaeological site is the arrangement of the various layers (strata) of earth and midden deposits on that site. In excavating, modern archaeologists pay careful attention to the location of each article found, in terms of its depth below the surface and also the layer, or stratum, in the excavation in which it is found. Not too many years ago, many archaeologists assumed that the Indians had not been here long: therefore, there would not be any stratigraphy on Indian sites; therefore, they did not look for any.

In 1932, Dr. William Ritchie, the great New York archaeologist, first used the word *Archaic* (*capital* A) to describe the culture that he had found in excavating the Lamoka Lake site by use of stratigraphic techniques. He found some sites which had no pottery and contained similar stone artifacts, and other sites in which Archaic strata were always *below* strata with pottery. He concluded that he had uncovered evidence of a very ancient and primitive culture in New York State. Through the years, more excavation was done in New York by Ritchie, who has personally been responsible for a tremendous amount of excellent archaeological work, leading to the reconstruction of the prehistory of nearly the entire state.

Other archaeologists digging elsewhere in the East began to find remains more or less similar to Ritchie's finds. It soon became apparent that a generally similar Archaic way of life spread across the whole East between 6000 B.C. and 1000 B.C. Then, study of excavations from all over the United States led archaeologists to the conclusion that there had been an Archaic *stage* of similar archaeological cultures throughout the whole of North America. In some places, such as in California, the Indians never progressed beyond the Archaic stage. In other areas, as in New York State, there was much development on the Archaic foundation. It was not until after 1950 that anyone realized just how old these old hunters really were. Dr. Carlyle Smith, who has done the major work in the metropolitan New York area, wrote in 1950 that the Archaic period ended about A.D. 700.

Not long after that, however, the carbon-14 dating

method was used on samples of ashes and charcoal collected from New York State Archaic sites. The results were startling. The early Archaic of upper New York was dated at 3433 B.C. ± 250, the Middle Archaic at 2980 B.C. ± 260, and the early portion of the following Early Woodland period dated at 998 B.C. ± 170! Now, an Archaic level in a site on the Hudson at Croton Point has been dated at about 4000 B.C., and a late Archaic site on Long Island at 1044 B.C. ± 300. The name Archaic is well applied to these hardy hunters of so long ago.

With all of this archaeological work as a foundation, it is possible to start tracing relationships between Archaic peoples in various parts of the East. The Archaic sites in metropolitan New York tell a story of trade or migrations from far-off areas. Traces of the early Lamoka Archaic culture appear in Grantville in the forms of narrow, side-notched arrowpoints.

Some archaeologists believe that the Lamoka culture entered New York from Kentucky and may be the Archaic culture of the people later known as the Iroquois tribes.

The Middle Archaic culture of New York State, called the Laurentian culture, also influenced the people of prehistoric New York as it spread down the Hudson Valley. While these influences came down the Hudson River other influences were brought up

54

and down the Atlantic coast by traders or migrants to and from the New York area and beyond. Projectile points, plummets, and bannerstones are quite similar as far down the coast as Virginia. The Archaic hunters may have been primitive, but we certainly can't say that they were completely isolated.

Around 1000 B.C. changes were abroad again in the Indian way of life. New influences, in the form of ideas and inventions, were trickling into the northeast coastal area from the South and West. Some were carried by traders, some possibly by war parties. Others simply passed from tribe to tribe. These influences reached our prehistoric New Yorkers in due time, and mingled with the old established Archaic way of life.

One of the first signs of this mingling is to be found in the New York City Archaic sites like the Weir Creek site and the Grantville site, where remains of large bowls made of steatite (soapstone) are found. These bowls were also found in the late Archaic cremation graves on Orient Point in eastern Long Island. Carved of a single piece of soapstone, the bowls are usually flat, oval in plan, with inverted lips and a "lug," or projecting handle, at each end. The bowls are generally found with a characteristic type of projectile point called the "Orient fishtail" by archaeologists because of the appearance of its base. Other arrowpoints and tools, such as rectangular

Stone Workers of the Forests

"celts," heavy stone adzes, are also found, while specific kinds of beads and stone neck ornaments called "gorgets" came into use.

These artifacts may have been introduced into the coastal regions from the South or West. At any rate, this final chapter of the Archaic, called the "Transitional Period" by some archaeologists, did not last long. For approximately a century, between about 1050 B.C. and 950 B.C., it can be recognized in Archaic sites and then it disappears, lost in the greater changes that were occurring as the Indians of New York and those of the East Coast in general embarked on a new venture, one of the most important steps in man's rise to civilization.

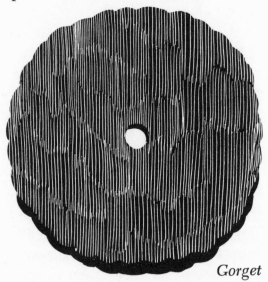

Gorget

3 · Stone Hoes and Potter's Paddles

THE OLD WOMAN sat before her hut in the bright afternoon sun of early fall. Her knotted fingers kneaded tirelessly at the great lump of grayish clay that sat on a flattened section of timber before her. Her eyes and thoughts were elsewhere: they were well occupied keeping watch on the naked children who scampered about among the bark-covered huts. A never-ending source of mischief! Why, if that little demon, Seagull, had not smashed their best cooking pot, she would not be here working on this clay!

From time to time she glanced wistfully down toward the shore where some of the younger folk were gathering shellfish and net-fishing to lay in supplies for the winter. She could see them splashing about in the water, and occasionally a snatch of laughter drifted up to her on the breeze. Once, she could have seen them clearly; then she would have been down there with them, packing as big a basket on her headband as any of the others, treading out the clams and oysters while the men poled and paddled their long dugout canoes across the river's calm surface.

Now, the figures and the canoes seemed hazy, indistinct. When she went into the water her legs ached.

If not in the water, she would have been in the fields, wielding a stone hoe among the carefully tended hills of corn, beans, and squash that were gradually swelling to harvest fullness there. But now her back ached when she bent over too long, and she tired rapidly in the heat of the sun. Better let the younger ones take the field chores, too. And so she sat around the huts, cooking for her eldest son, watching the children, and doing other odd jobs— such as making pottery. At this she was a recognized expert—even the years had not touched her skill with the clay.

After the pot had been broken, she had taken her basket and a hoe, and hurried off to the shore, where the sea had uncovered a bank of good clay. The basket filled with chunks of the greasy gray material, she had hurried home and settled before her board to pick out the larger bits of rocks, plant roots, and minerals contained in the clay. When the whole lump of clay had been carefully picked over, she had added some water and kneaded the clay to the right consistency. Then she collected some coarse sand from the beach and mixed this into the clay. If this was not added, the pot would explode in the firing!

Now her sensitive fingers told her that the sand had been pretty well mixed through the clay and she was ready to start the pot. A shout brought the young granddaughter on the run. A curious girl, she wanted to know all about woman's work. She would be a good potter too someday!

Deftly, the old woman shaped from a ball of clay a little conical bowl about a hand's length across. "This is how you begin," she said. Then she began to make long snakelike rolls of the soft clay, rolling it with her hand on the board surface. The deft old fingers smoothed one of the rolls onto the rim of the little bowl, making it higher and wider. Then another roll, and another followed. The bowl grew with each coil. The clay rolls were first pressed into place from the top; then the crevices between them were filled

in and smoothed over by excess clay. The little girl
sat fascinated as the pot grew into a wide, straight-
sided vessel with tapering pointed bottom.

"The paddle!" The old lady spoke, motioning toward the hut. In a moment it was in her hand: a short
wooden paddle wrapped with coarse twine made of
tough twisted vegetable fiber. Taking a smooth
beach stone from beside the board, she placed the
pot on its side. She held the beach stone against the
inside of the pot and began to beat gently with the
paddle on the outside, directly over the stone. The
stone and the paddle moved slowly over the surface
of the pot, driving together the coils of clay until the
walls of the pot were a solid mass of clay, and the

whole outside surface was covered with the impressions of the cord wrapping on the paddle.

"So! Do you think you will make pottery as good as mine someday?" asked the old woman. To the wide-eyed girl's eager nod, she laughed: "Wait till we fire it when it has dried a bit! You can help me stack the wood—but *only if you do as I say!*"

When archaeologists speak of periods of time or cultures, they are not talking about things that somehow existed for the peoples of the past. The Indians of the Archaic period did not call themselves by that name. The evidence for these periods, or cultures, is not clearly shown in the sites of ancient camps on helpful little signs saying "Made by Woodland Indians—500 B.C." The periods of time and archaeological cultures into which an archaeologist organizes his finds are the results of his *own* brain work. After carefully studying the artifacts that he has found, their stratigraphic positions in various sites, the carbon-14 dates associated with these sites, and all the other evidence of such things as animal bones, plant remains, and geology, it is the archaeologist who must at last decide how to divide up his finds in terms of time and space. If he has 10,000 years of history recorded in his sites, he must decide at what points in that span of time to draw major dividing lines. If he has a series of sites in a particular period that are somewhat different from other sites of the same period, he must decide whether or not they are sufficiently different to warrant naming this series as representative of a different archaeological culture. Dividing a sequence into time periods is usually done on the basis of major breaks or changes in the way of life of a people, such as the change evident between the nomadic, Clovis point-making, big-game hunters of Paleo-Indian times, and the more settled small-game hunters of the Archaic.

Marked changes in the tool kits of ancient peoples also give archaeologists handy signposts in time on which to pin period names. Such changes might be the appearance of pottery in an archaeological culture that had not made it before, or the appearance of new types of pottery much different than those found in earlier sites or older strata. Where pottery was made, it provides a good yardstick for archaeologists, who mark off their time units by the changes that occurred in the shape, size, decoration, or finish of the pottery of the ancient inhabitants. In other areas of the world, or in times such as the Archaic of New York where pottery was lacking, time periods are marked off by changes in the forms of spearheads, and other stone and bone implements of various types.

Time periods are really artificial divisions: things just don't happen like that in real life. People do not recognize abrupt changes of the type marked off on archaeological charts, based on pottery and stone tools. For them, the important things are likely to be customs, ceremonies, religious beliefs, the rules of chiefs, or the relations between clans or tribes.

Resemblances between sites must be done on a "majority rule" basis: sites that share *many* or *very important* common characteristics in a particular period are grouped together. Those that are unusual are separated and given different titles. This sort of thing happened in upper New York during the Archaic period when there were different kinds of Archaic cultures in different parts of the state, and the Archaic people of prehistoric New York City shared a jumble of artifacts from most of them.

The end of the Archaic period and the beginning of the following period in the New York City area—called the Woodland period—is very clearly marked in the archaeological record by the appearance of a particular kind of artifact—pottery. There are other signs of the ending of the Archaic period that are less obvious than the evidence of jagged, thick fragments of crude pottery, but nonetheless very important—more important than pottery itself in terms of their meaning for the lives of the prehistoric New Yorkers. These are the signs of the introduction of agriculture. However, because pottery fragments are the most frequently found artifacts on these Woodland sites,

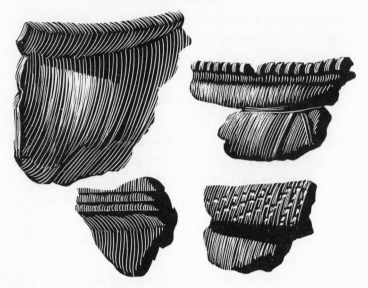

and because the changes in pottery composition, shape, and decoration have been found to occur in a regular way through time, the rest of the story of prehistoric New York will be tied to the pottery "yardstick," as will be explained in more detail later.

It seems likely that the Archaic people were basically the same people as those of the Woodland period. There was probably not any invasion of outsiders bringing ideas and inventions with them. What seems to have happened is that the Archaic culture just had things added to it and finally ceased to be "Archaic" as a result of the additions.

The campsites of the early Woodland New Yorkers were generally located along the shore. Villages sprung up overlooking bays, on little inlets, or on points. Villages were also found near streams and far inland in other parts of the region. Sites of this period are at North Beach, where La Guardia Airport now stands, Throgs Neck, Pelham Bay Park, Dyckman Street, and on Staten Island. Just outside the metropolitan area, a site was located on Matinecock Point, and another in Glen Cove. The villages of the Woodland Indians were probably not much different from those of their Archaic ancestors. They seem to have inhabited round or oval houses made of light poles planted in the ground, and bent and lashed into a framework probably thatched with grass, reed mats, or bark. When the houses were abandoned or moved, the imprint left by the removal of the poles, or the rotting poles themselves, remained in the soil. Thousands of years later, archaeologists can identify the dark round spots left in the earth by such post molds. Unfortunately, in New York City, it has been impossible to trace out the outline of a complete house as yet.

Scattered around the houses were shallow saucer-shaped pits—some containing hearths for cooking and others used for the disposal of refuse. There were also midden heaps, with the usual mixture of shells, bones, charcoal, ash, and artifacts of all types discarded by their long-dead owners.

In these midden heaps are found traces of the most

important of the changes that transformed the way of life of the Archaic into the Woodland way of life: the remains of agricultural food plants. Charred corn and beans, still recognizable, were found in refuse deposits at the 2,900-year-old Matinecock site! Tobacco was also being grown: this can be deduced from a fragment of a tobacco pipe found on one of the early Woodland sites in the New York City area.

This evidence of farming may not seem very important to us, who are so used to agricultural food that we take it for granted. However, anyone who has ever had to survive for any time on the food provided by hunting and gathering wild plants will realize just how handy it is to be able to grow one's meals. In the first place, agriculture permits, and almost *forces,* people to live a settled existence. They don't have to be off in the woods chasing game and hunting for new stands of wild berries or groves of nut trees. They must stick close to their fields throughout the planting and harvesting seasons to protect them from drought, weeds, wild animals, or human intruders.

Another benefit of agriculture is that it generally allows people to produce a surplus of food—more than they themselves can eat. This is valuable in many ways. First, it permits people to think about things other than struggling to stay alive—things such as inventing new tools and implements, trying some new kind of stone or wood, thinking of better songs, chants, or magic. Then, a surplus also makes the tribal leaders a bit more important. The chiefs usually control the tribal lands in some way and they get back part of the food surplus in return. This surplus they control for their own purposes. They can reward with it, support the poorer tribesmen, use it to give feasts, or pay craftsmen for ornaments or special tools. And so the social organization of primitive agricultural people begins to develop.

In the New York area, agriculture arrived on the scene about 900 B.C. or later. In the remote Near East, however, agriculture had at that time been an established way of life for many thousands of years.

Stone Hoes and Potter's Paddles

About 7000 B.C. evidence of the first agriculture in the world and use of domestic animals is found in the ruins of ancient villages in the hills of Iran, and in the remains of little towns far down inside the huge mound of the city of Jericho. Upon this agricultural foundation the civilizations of Sumer, Akkad, Babylon, and Egypt had flowered and already waned when the prehistoric New Yorkers first found out about planting their corn and beans.

This new way of getting food did not produce any earth-shaking changes at first. Paleo-botanists (those who study ancient and extinct forms of plant life) have found pollen grains of a species of wild corn that existed on the East Coast as far back as sixty thousand years ago. These pollen grains were found deep in peat bogs on Cape Cod. Somewhere, very likely in southern or southwestern North America or possibly even down in Mexico, some Indian group or individual discovered that corn could be planted. (Wild corn had probably been eaten for a long time.) The way of doing this was passed from tribe to tribe by traders, captives, etc., and finally spread into northeastern North America, reaching our early New Yorkers. The secrets of planting squash and beans may have been passed on from outside the area. Squash, at least, seems to have been domesticated by early Indians in our deep South.

The practice of agriculture may not have been

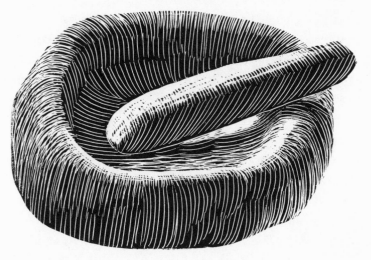

widely accepted at first—old ways of life die hard, and hunting was still very important, but gradually more and more Indians were clearing fields, planting, and harvesting. Over the course of many years, the Woodland Indians became farmers. As a result of agriculture, a new type of tool was developed: a crude stone hoe, made of a flat piece of stone, meant to be used on a wooden handle. The corn was ground with mortars and pestles similar to those used by the Archaic people for fruits and berries, although stone mortars were also used, made of large stones with deep depressions in the center.

The men of the Woodland period did not, by any means, give up their hunting to tend the fields. They undoubtedly put in their share of time in the gardens, clearing the plots and burning them, and possibly at harvest time, but it is likely that the women did much of the field labor. The men went about their hunting as usual, with the same kinds of spears and spear throwers used by their late Archaic ancestors. They were also equipped with a new and more deadly weapon, the bow and arrow. The small projectile points found in early Woodland sites seem to indicate that the prehistoric New Yorkers got this valuable weapon at that time.

The points were mainly of quartz, the most abundant local stone useful for that purpose. Others were made of bone, with toothed edges, and must have been wicked weapons. Hunting was made easier by the use of the dogs which seem to have been fairly numerous around Indian villages. The animals were also used for food on occasion, as shown by cooked dog-bone fragments in shell middens. Dogs were not the only unusual mammals eaten by prehistoric New Yorkers: man himself also provided a meal on occasion. I recall once seeing fragments of cooked human bone in a box of miscellaneous bones picked up by an amateur archaeologist working at Pelham Bay Park.

Fish and shellfish were still important and always would be for the New Yorkers, who never overlooked the riches of the sea in their diet. Stone net-weights show that netting was still popular, and fish bones are plentiful in the middens.

Bone fishhooks, shaped much like our metal varieties, may have been first dangled into the waters around Manhattan during this period. These objects have been found in some sites with early Woodland pottery: it is not certain that the pottery and the hooks were deposited at the same time.

The stone tools of the Woodland tool kit were very much the same as those of the Archaic period. There were grooved axes and celts for woodworking, hunting, and warfare. Stone knives and drills were used in working wood and bone. Antler wedges were used to split wood, and stone tools were sometimes set in antler sockets in wooden handles. On the basis of what we know of primitive people still existing in remote

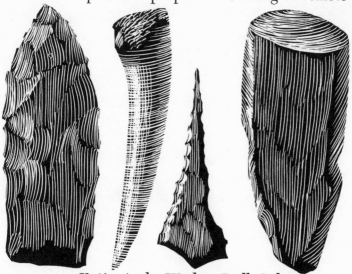

Knife, Antler Wedge, Drill, Celt

parts of the world, we can assume that the Woodland people had a lot of wooden implements and decorations: bowls, platters, dishes, spoons, ladles, paddles, perhaps masks, and idols, and any number of things. None of these, of course, survived and so we can only guess, on the basis of the tools that we find.

The Woodland people made use of bone and antler for all types of implements. Large quantities of bone splinters with sharp polished tips were found in sites of this period, such as the Matinecock Point site. These were used as awls for punching holes in skins or thin wood or bark, and perhaps also used in attaching the thatch or bark covering to house frames. The well-dressed Indian of the early Woodland period must have looked a great deal like his Archaic ancestors in winter, clad in fur clothing which was probably fitted for warmth. Summer clothing may have been light: a breechcloth of skin or coarse woven cloth, and a robe of skin. Cloth weaving is another invention that seems to have come into the New York area around this time. Its presence can be detected from impressions left in the clay of pottery, which was pressed with paddles wrapped in cloth on occasion, as well as with cord-wrapped paddles. Women probably wore skirts of skins or cloth and robes of fur, and may have dressed more like the men in winter. We know that Woodland people had face and body paints, since brown and red clay and minerals used for these purposes have been found in the sites around New York. Ornaments were made of animal teeth, bone tube beads, and polished stone.

Excavating the campsites of the early Woodland people, archaeologists have found not only the remains of fires, houses, and tools of all sorts, but the remains of the people themselves. In some cases, the dead were buried quite close to village sites, often in trash pits or trash heaps or in sandy soil deposits. These pits may have been used in winter when the undisturbed soil was frozen too solidly for the wooden or stone digging tools of the Indians to break through. The number of burials in such pits, however, has not been large, and it is clear that many Indian burials were made elsewhere, in the beaches or in glacial sand deposits where digging was easy all year round. Some of the dead were buried in what archaeologists call the "flexed" position, with knees drawn up tightly to chest. In other cases, the body was allowed to decay; then the bones were cleaned and packed away into the earth in a tight bundle. Ornaments or tools were apparently placed with some of the burials, although this is not certain, because the burial in question was excavated long ago, and the notes of the archaeologist are not clear on the matter.

Aside from the information on burials, there is very little to go on in trying to reconstruct native religion. There are no stone idols or figures of any type made at this time, or no suspicious looking difficult-to-explain artifacts that might be religious. It is quite likely that the religion of the Woodland people was not much different from that of the earlier or later periods. A study of the religion of the Eastern Indians at the arrival of the white man, and the few remnants of Eastern tribes that still existed into the twentieth century, indicates that religion all over the East among the Algonkian-language tribes (of which the New Yorkers are members) was pretty much the same. Their religion was based on belief in a large number of animal or natural spirits of various types and a few high-ranking spirits. Much of the religion had to do with success in hunting, planting, and war, and it is likely that it was the same for the Woodland people.

Back in the early years of the twentieth century archaeologists did their digging in a somewhat helter-skelter fashion. They were more concerned with finding things than they were with where the things they found were located in the sites, and how these finds were related to each other. They were also inclined to pay less attention to the crude kinds of implements and utensils found. The beautiful banner-stones, the highly polished axes and celts, and the neatly chipped arrow and spearpoints were what interested them.

Because of this, the importance of pottery for archaeology was overlooked for quite some time. Drs. Skinner and Parker had broken down the pottery of New York State into three main types—a crude variety which they called "Algonkian," a better-made variety called "Iroquois," and a type that stood mid-way between the two in terms of crudity, called "sub-Iroquois." The Algonkian was the oldest, the Iroquois the most recent. These archaeologists cared more about the pottery that had decorations on it, and often discarded undecorated fragments that they found.

In upper New York State, however, Dr. William Ritchie, a student of Parker's, went much further than his teacher in his archaeological research and analysis. We have already seen how Ritchie actually "discovered" the Archaic period with his work in New York in the 1920's and 30's. At the same time, he was also working out the later periods of New York prehistory, and paying a great deal of close attention to the details of *all* the pottery found. He was soon able to identify specific types of pottery, distinguished by decoration, shape, and other features, and associated with various archaeological cultures in New York's past.

In the early 1930's, a new archaeologist picked up the threads of the investigations of New York prehistory where Skinner had left off. This was Carlyle

Smith, now an archaeologist at the University of Kansas. Smith began his work as a student, working along with other students and amateurs in the Long Island area, and cooperating with the Flushing Historical Society and the Long Island chapter of the New York State Archaeological Society. By the beginning of World War II, Smith's excavations and studies of archaeological collections were extensive. On the basis of this work he was fitting together, bit by bit, a picture of the prehistory of coastal New York. After service in the Army Air Force during the war, Smith returned to Columbia University as a Ph.D. candidate, and resumed his study of the archaeology of coastal New York, to present his findings as his doctoral dissertation.

Smith's research took him to the dusty storerooms of the American Museum of Natural History, the Museum of the American Indian, and the Peabody Museum at Yale. He studied again the collections of amateurs and other archaeologists who worked in the area and he had his own extensive collections to use.

It was a very difficult task. The collections were all fairly small: no large-scale excavations had ever really been done around New York City. The collections made by Skinner, and by M. R. Harrington, an archaeologist who worked around New York in the early 1900's, were difficult to use. The notes made by these men were not always very clear or detailed.

Further, they had often thrown away parts of the collections.

All was not lost, however, for in some cases the excavators had recorded the depth beneath the surface of the ground at which potsherds (fragments of pottery vessels), projectile points, and stone tools had been found. Also, they had kept separate the contents of various ancient refuse pits that they had found. These records helped, for they allowed Smith to determine which kinds of pottery and stone tools were earlier and which later on some sites, and indicated which kinds of artifacts were of the same age, being found in the same pits or the same levels of particular sites.

Smith saw the value of the thick, crude, roughly finished potsherds. He realized what they could mean for archaeological dating. In other parts of the United States and the world, new techniques had been developed for analyzing pottery and Smith began to apply them to see if they could help further classify the collections he was studying.

He tried to identify pottery *types* in the collections. That is, he tried to find particular combinations of decorations, shapes, surface finishes, and clays that would always appear together on the same pot. When he found a set of characteristics that always appeared together, he would label it a type.

The type name consisted of two parts: usually the

name of the site where this kind of pottery was most frequent, such as "Matinecock," "North Beach," etc., and a descriptive term to indicate the kind of finish or decoration found on the pottery, such as "cord-marked," "stamped," etc.

This does not mean that the Indians regarded it as a type of pottery. We do not know what the Indians thought about various kinds of pots, nor will we ever know. Smith was looking for types that had *historical* meaning only; that is, types that were useful archaeologically for marking off time periods. In some cases, he could determine how useful these types were from the strata in which they were found on the various sites.

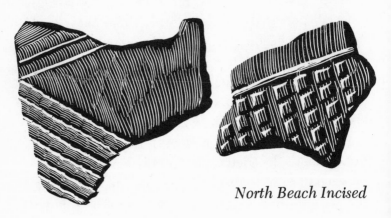

North Beach Incised

Matinecock Stamped

80

In other parts of the world, particularly in Peru and in the Mississippi Valley, pottery-type analysis had proven very useful in dating. It was found that pottery that had been excavated or collected from the surfaces of sites in these areas could be analyzed by types. If properly identified, the types of pottery would be seen to change in their proportions to each other through time and from site to site. In one period, type A might represent 75 percent of all pottery found, while in the next period it would only make up 50 percent, and later only 30 percent. At the same time, pottery type B might be gradually increasing in proportion as pottery type A decreased.

Using information on the percentages of the different types of pottery found in a number of sites, an archaeologist can work out the relative age of the sites. That is, he can tell which site is oldest, which is most recent, and which is of medium age, just from the pottery-type percentages. This is done by a complicated technique called "site seriation." The archaeologist doing a seriation uses a long strip of graph paper to represent each site. On the graph-paper strip, percentages of pottery types are shown by black bars of appropriate lengths. The archaeologist moves these strips around on a large chart until the pattern of the bar graphs shows a pattern of types gradually increasing and decreasing in percentages relative to each other. Experience has shown that

81

seriation of ceramic traits in New York	plain		cord marked		brushed		incised		stamped			
site 1	▄		▄				▄		▄			
site 2	▄		▄	▄					▄			
site 3	▄				▄		▄		▄			
site 4			▄		▄		▄					
site 5	▄				▄		▄		▄			

certain graph patterns will appear and these are what the archaeologist is looking for. "Seriation" is not only done with pottery fragments: it has been done in the United States with arrow heads, in Alaska with archaeological harpoon heads, and I was able to do it in Polynesia with ancient mother-of-pearl fishhooks and files made of coral branches.

For good site seriation, however, an archaeologist needs lots of sites—say sixty or seventy or more—and lots of potsherds from each site—about two to three hundred. Smith's collections were unfortunately few in number and all small.

But this did not stop him. He did a similar kind of analysis in which he traced the changes in the various *characteristics* of pottery instead of the pottery *types*. He made tables and graphs showing the percentages of potsherds that had different kinds of finish—plain, cord-marked, brushed, etc., and the kinds of decoration. He also counted up the sherds that contained shell mixed in the clay as opposed to those that contained crushed rock or sand to keep the pot from exploding when fired. He found that these characteristics changed through time: in earlier sites, crushed rock was mixed in the clay for "temper" more frequently, while in later sites shell was used. In late sites more sherds had plain finishes, while in early sites more had cord markings from the cord-wrapped paddles used in pot manufacture.

Smith had done a seriation, not on types, but on characteristics. He had found a way to wring more information out of the pottery that earlier archaeologists had found useless and uninteresting. This is a good example of the application of observation in scientific method. Sometimes the most uninviting and commonplace things will yield all kinds of information if we only work hard at trying to find it.

On the basis of his pottery analysis, Smith set up a series of periods for Woodland prehistory in the New York area. He could determine which sites fell in which periods by the kinds and characteristics of pottery they contained. In the rest of this book we will use names of periods and types that Smith estab-

83

lished in his report of 1950, which has become a "bible" for every coastal New York archaeologist.

The pottery of the earlier part of the Woodland period around New York City is known as pottery of the "Windsor tradition." The name *Windsor* comes from a site in Connecticut: at this time, pottery from the New York City area right into central Connecticut was all basically alike. Therefore the general kind of pottery was called the "Windsor tradition." Within the "tradition," many types could be identified.

The earliest Woodland pottery in the New York area, as found in the shell middens at North Beach, Matinecock Point, Pelham, and other sites, is very crude and unattractive. The pots were usually straight-sided with pointed bottoms. The clay is thick, soft, and often crumbly, showing evidence that the Indian potters were not too careful in binding together the coils in the vessels that they made.

The decoration of the Windsor potters was not much to behold: little holes were stamped into the wet clay, singly or in series, scallopshell edges were also used to impress decorative marks in the pots, fibers were dragged over the surface to give a "brushed" effect, or designs were cut in with a sharp tool. These decorations were all combined in straight-line designs around the upper part of the pot and look as though they might be designs borrowed from

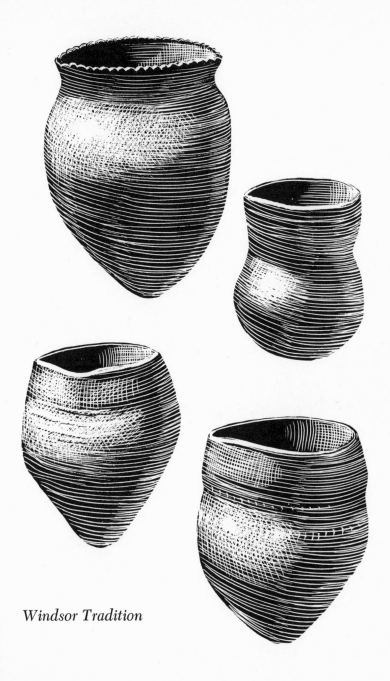

Windsor Tradition

basketry of which the Woodland people undoubtedly had a great deal.

A common type is called "Vinette Interior Cord-Marked," nearly identical to the Vinette I pottery from upper New York State. This type is undecorated, and is covered, both inside and out, with markings from the cord-wrapped potter's paddle. Another early type is "North Beach Brushed," similar in many ways to Vinette, but having light brush marks all over the outside surface of the pot. Yet another type, somewhat later in time than those previously mentioned, is known as "Clearview Stamped." These pots are again thick-walled with pointed bottoms. They have a bumpy surface, into which was stamped many short series of impressions made with a toothed

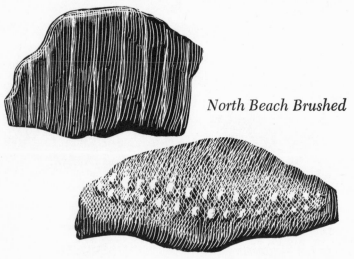

North Beach Brushed

instrument. The pots were probably used for cooking over an open fire, as many of the potsherds still bear charred food remains on the inside from a succession of Indian stews that were never scoured out. The pointed base was probably set in a hole or propped up by stones. On the other hand, the contents of the pot might have been heated by dropping in rocks, heated to a high temperature in a fire. "Stone-boiling," as this technique is called, can heat food rapidly, and was used all over the world.

The New York area is today the crossroads of many foreign influences, and so it was, to a much less extent, even far back in the days before Christ. Just now, a picture is beginning to emerge of foreign influences entering into the New York area not only in the Archaic period but in the Woodland as well.

In Ohio, Kentucky, Indiana, and nearby states during the early Woodland period, a strange culture appeared. This is known as the Adena culture, and it is really better known for its cult of the dead than for its other aspects. The Adena people, whoever they were, buried their dead in low mounds raised over the remains of houses. These houses were built in an unusual pattern that is typical of Adena culture: pairs of posts were arranged in a circle around four central posts. Some of the dead were buried with large quantities of grave offerings, including beads made of cold-hammered nugget copper, stone or

87

copper "gorgets" (possibly neck ornaments or a special kind of spearthrower weight), tubular pipes, tablets of stone engraved with strange snake, bird, or flower patterns, large numbers of stone blades, and "birdstones"—strange little popeyed birdlike sculptures that also may have been used on spear throwers. Evidence has been building up to show that the Adena people, or at least some of them, moved out of their home territory toward the East after 900 B.C. Some Adena people moved into the Chesapeake Bay area around the beginning of the Christian era, but apparently other Adena groups arrived in upper New York State between 900 B.C. and 500 B.C., affecting the local Indian groups there a great deal. Ritchie has shown that many Adena implements and ornaments are found in New York early Woodland sites, many of them made of stone that can be identified as coming from Ohio. There is not much evidence that Adena people moved into the New York City area, but an Adena-like birdstone was found in a Throgs Neck site in 1955, and another had been found long ago by Skinner near Spuyten Duyvil. This is no proof that Adena people, with their strange religious cult of the dead, were in the area, because birdstones are also found in upper New York, and the Throgs Neck and Spuyten Duyvil finds could just have been traded down the Hudson, as so much else seems to have been.

While Adena was still flourishing in Ohio, another burial-mound culture, called the Hopewell culture, also arose there in about 300 B.C. The Hopewellians were not second-best to the Adena people in their elaborate burials. Their dead were buried dressed in fine ornaments of shell, stone, and metal, surrounded by all sorts of tools and implements, and often walled in with timbers to protect them from the earth. One of the characteristic grave offerings of the Hopewell people was seashells from Florida.

In digging on a large Indian site near Tottenville on the tip of Staten Island, a probable Hopewell burial (without a mound) was uncovered by a Columbia University archaeology student, Jerome Jacobson. In the grave, the body of a six-year-old child was found, a child that must have been well-loved. The little skull was surrounded with a circle of large flint blades. Around the neck was a necklace of shells of a type found in the Gulf of Mexico (Olivella and Marginella shells). A copper gorget and a highly polished stone pipe completed the grave offerings. Jacobson correctly states that this is one of the most striking examples of Hopewell influence to appear on the northeast coast. What was this little child doing on Staten Island so long ago? Was he the child of an important Hopewell trader or refugee chief? A captive from a war raid to the west? An immigrant? We will never know. And we can only guess at the labor involved in producing the possessions that went with the little stranger to the other world. We can, however, be glad that the careful work done on Staten Island has placed his long-lost grave on the pages of the archaeological record so that it may help us puzzle out the tangled prehistory of the great city of New York.

The life of the prehistoric New Yorkers remained much the same throughout the centuries before and after the time of Christ. A few new types of tools were invented, and different shapes and kinds of decoration were developed by potters for their vessels. The harvests improved slowly and life went on much as it had for centuries. The middle Woodland period was really not very much different from the early Woodland in terms of the kind of life that people led.

By about A.D. 1000, however, changes again are seen in the archaeological record. This time they are most visible in pottery, the archaeologists' best way of detecting culture change. The pottery of the Windsor tradition suddenly disappears from the sites around New York City and a new type of pottery appears in its place. The new pottery is, of course, very important, but what is most important is what the new pottery *means*: who made it, where it came from, what it is related to, and what happened to the Windsor pottery. In the next chapter, we will discuss these questions.

4 · Invasions or Inventions?

THE WAILING had been going on night and day for two days; even the bright sunlight and clear winter skies did not seem to melt the sadness that hung like an invisible curtain about the huts. Winter was always a bad time; one expected that some of the old ones would go to the spirit world, and some of the young ones, too. The cold and damp seemed too much for them to take. But to lose two at once, in the same hut! Everyone was very sad and there were some who muttered darkly about unhappy spirits and witchcraft, but few would listen to them.

Old Moon-at-Harvest had become ill right after the first cold snap. She had gone out in the fierce wind and snow to pick up firewood and had not returned. Her son, Puma, had followed her wandering tracks as soon as he realized how long she had been gone and found her, lying where she had fainted in the snow, beneath a load of faggots. Her face was blue with cold and she did not speak. When they got her to the hut and warmed her by the fire, she awoke, but could not speak clearly or move well. Then came

91

the coughing and sneezing, and soon her brow got hot and dry. Sometimes she babbled.

Puma's infant son, the delight of his grandmother's eye, would not leave her side, running to her every chance he got, though his parents scolded him. Then he, too, began to burn with fever and cough.

It was not long before Moon-at-Harvest quietly went to sleep forever. Puma awoke one night and realized that her rattling, rasping breathing had stopped. He moved silently across the hut in the gloom and felt the cold forehead. The next day the infant was gone, too. Puma sat with a frozen face. The women would weep enough for him. A warrior could not show the deep wound in his heart at the loss of his first-born son and his mother.

And so, when the prayers had been said and the feast of the dead made, the still forms were dressed and bundled up, knees to chest, in layers of matting. One of the large trash pits at the edge of the village was selected for the grave. The soil was sandy there: the stone hoes could not penetrate the solid crust of frozen earth elsewhere. A small pit was dug into the refuse and the mat bundles were laid side by side at the bottom to the wail of the magician. He called on the spirits of the dead to leave their former dwellings without harming the survivors, and go happily to the spirit world. A fragment of a pot was thrown in—a favorite toy of the child.

94

Invasions or Inventions?

Then the pit was filled in slowly with baskets of trash from the funeral feast and the ashes of the cooking fire, while Puma stood by. The grave was no sooner closed than he went to work with some of the men of the family. Out in the forest, they gathered small saplings, several inches in diameter, lopping the branches off with sure strokes of their stone axes. These poles were then driven through the thin top-soil around the grave into the sandy soil beneath, to form posts for a fence. Between these posts were woven tree branches and entire small saplings and shrubs. At least when the wolves prowled the village in the icy winter nights they would not disturb the last resting places of Puma's loved ones.

This sad story is, of course, purely imaginary, for no archaeologist can know about the details of the human beings who were part of the past that he is studying. Nevertheless, there is a factual basis for the whole story, for a burial, containing the bodies of an old woman and a child, was excavated in an old Indian refuse pit in a village site not far from Jamaica Bay at Aqueduct, Queens County. The excavation was done in 1939 by Dr. Ralph Solecki, a well-known archaeologist who began his excavations in the Long Island–New York City area and has since moved to the trail of Neanderthal men and early farmers in the hills of Iraq, and Paleo-Indians in Alaska. Solecki and a group from the Flushing Historical Society

East River Tradition

carefully excavated the pit and its pathetic contents, uncovering and mapping the location of the fourteen postholes that encircled the grave.

The pottery fragments in the pit were of the same general kind as those found in other parts of the village site. These were thinner, harder, more well-made pots of a kind known generally as pottery of the "East River tradition." East River pottery presents quite an interesting problem for the archaeologists of the East Coast.

The East River tradition pottery is, as the name implies, different from that of the Windsor tradition in a number of important ways. Dr. Smith spotted these differences in his careful study of pottery of the New York City area. This new pottery, however, does not just appear at one or two sites and then vanish: it appears at all of the late Woodland sites around New York City and completely takes the place of the Windsor pottery.

This seems to have occurred at about A.D. 1100 or A.D. 1200 or so, judging from carbon-14 dates obtained from related sites in upper New York and Connecticut.

At Grantville, the Archaic levels are covered by deposits bearing East River pottery, and the same occurs at Dyckman Street. The new pottery is found at Clason Point, Throgs Neck, Van Cortlandt and Pelham Bay parks in the Bronx, and at Aqueduct, Port Washington, and Dosoris Pond on Long Island. Staten Island was also inhabited by East River pottery makers, who left remains at Bowman's Brook.

In contrast to the thick, often crumbly, efforts of the Windsor potters, with their childish decoration, the East River pottery is more attractive. East River pots, regardless of type, have thin, hard walls that have been well worked over by hands and paddles. Many East River types of pottery have cord-marking around the bottom of the pot, but many also have smooth, plain surfaces, the cord-marking having been completely rubbed out. Some East River pots are like the Windsor pots in shape, with conical bottoms and straight sides. Others, however, are much more elaborate. The lips of the pots are sometimes rolled outward, and in some later types the whole shape of the vessel is changed: a round-bottomed pot was produced with a narrow neck and a thick collar around the opening. The neck and collar of the East River pot was the place where the potter chose to display her artistry. She marked geometric designs around the upper part of the pot with a number of different kinds of tools. Sometimes a sharpened stick, a comb, or a bone awl was used to scratch the clay; on other occasions, the edge of the cord-wrapped potters' paddle was used to impress a series of lines into the clay, while a few pots were marked with lines of little indentations, made with a toothed shell disc, much like a gear. The decoration was nearly always geometric, composed of series of straight lines running parallel, or criss-crossing each other at angles. These decorations ran around the neck or collar of the pot in a continuous band, or in a series of separate designs.

A well-known type that appears fairly early in the East River period is that which Smith called "Bowman's Brook Incised," after the Staten Island site where it had been found in such quantity by Dr. Skinner between 1903 and 1907. Bowman's Brook Incised was also found at the Aqueduct site by Dr. Solecki and his party. This kind of pottery has very little cord-marking on the outside, and the pot itself is rather egg-shaped. Around the rim of the pot designs were cut into the still-damp clay. These consist of triangles and rectangles "hanging" from the rim of the pot, filled with incised lines in parallel or herringbone arrangement. Sometimes little blobs of clay were applied to the neck of the pot and modeled in the form of humanlike faces.

Another type is called "Clason's Point Stamped" after the Bronx site where large quantities of it were dug from fifty-nine refuse pits and a broad midden deposit situated on high ground near a cove. This type of pottery is characterized by a globular body with a narrow neck and a collar around the opening. The lower part of the body of the pot is usually covered with cord-marking, but the neck and collar is smooth. The Indian potter chose a scallop shell as a decorative tool, pressing the edge of the shell into the collar and neck of the pot to form rippling lines that run around the collar horizontally or cross it vertically and diagonally.

Some of the most handsome pottery of the East River tradition is that called "Eastern Incised," another round-bottomed type with narrow neck and collar. Into the collars of Eastern Incised pots were cut geometric designs of all kinds—nests of diamonds, one inside the other, sawtooth designs made of rows of triangles, and sometimes the same little faces noted on the Bowman's Brook pottery.

East River people also made their smoking pipes

Bowman's Brook Incised

Clason Point Stamped

Eastern Incised

of pottery, decorated with designs of the same sort found on the large pots. Two types of pipes were used: one was straight and tapered from the bowl to the mouthpiece. It would have been smoked like a big clay cigar. The other kind of pipe used by the East River people was more like modern pipes in its "elbow" shape. Both varieties must have been rather hot to handle and certainly would not delight the pipesmokers of today, who like cool-smoking pipes with all sorts of filtering devices attached. But, then, remember that the Indians did not use tobacco in the way that we do in twentieth century America. It was part of the ritual in ceremonies of various kinds. Men smoked occasionally, but probably not more than once or twice a day, for relaxation. The strong tobacco may not have been well-dried when it was smoked and very likely produced mild dizziness and a feeling of well-being.

Tobacco and its use among the Indians is a very interesting subject, but it should not draw us away from an equally interesting subject, one that tells a lot about archaeology, archaeologists, and how they think: the East River pottery and where it came from.

When a new kind of pottery appears in an archaeological site, the archaeologist has two main choices to make: did the pottery come from elsewhere, or was it just a nice, new kind, invented by

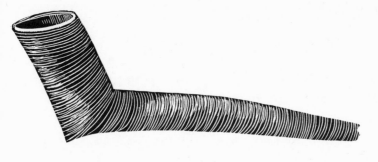

the people who had been living there all along? A third choice is a combination of the two: some of the ideas and ways of making the pottery came from elsewhere, were picked up by the people who had been living there all along, and worked into a new and different kind of pottery.

Obviously the first thing an archaeologist does is to look around at nearby areas to see where other similar pottery might have been found. Smith did this: he found similar pottery in New Jersey in sites along the Delaware River. Also, he noted that pottery very much like the East River pottery in shape and design was found in upper New York State in the archaeological culture called Owasco, which appears at about the same time that the East River pottery appears in New York. Other East River pottery resembles the later Iroquois pottery of central and northern New York State. As a matter of fact, pottery that roughly resembles East River in its overall design is found throughout most of the northeast. The Windsor pottery, although no longer found in the New York area, continued on eastern Long Island and in Connecticut right along with the East River pottery in the Manhattan area.

This presents a real problem to an archaeologist: how do you decide where East River pottery came from if the pottery in all the surrounding areas is pretty much like it, except for details of thickness, decoration, and finish? To make matters worse, the Indian pottery of the Northeast is all pretty crude compared to that produced in Ohio, for example, or the beautifully painted pots of the prehistoric Southwest. Each Indian potter made her own pots as best she could: some potters were good, others bad, and many in between. Pots found on the same site differ a lot in terms of quality of workmanship, even when of the same type. There was no such thing as the "mass production" and "design specifications" of modern industry for Indian potters. They did not even use any kind of obvious "trademark."

And so, well-made pots from a site in Massachusetts might look like well-made pots from New

Jersey. Poorly made pots from New York City might resemble poorly made pots from other sites in New York State. But does this mean that there is some kind of connection between those pots or does it mean that, just by chance, Indian potters working miles apart happened to produce pots that were very much alike, once in a while?

Smith's task again was not an easy one: he searched the archaeological reports and studied collections. Finally, he decided that the East River people probably came from the Delaware River valley, to the northwest of the metropolitan area. Pottery found on sites over there seemed to be ancestral to the East River pottery. Further, we know that when the Europeans arrived the Delawares were holding the west side of the Hudson and Staten Island. What could be more natural than to expect that the East River pottery was a result of a group moving in from New Jersey?

In 1955, I excavated a site in Connecticut, a large midden located on a beautiful point jutting into Long Island Sound. On smogless days I could see the skyscrapers of Manhattan very clearly. This turned out to be an early East River site, but it contained a surprise. Windsor pottery was also there, mixed in with the East River! It looked as though the people who lived on my site had been using both kinds of pottery.

Invasions or Inventions?

Now Smith had not found any clear-cut evidence of this in the metropolitan area. It seemed to him that Windsor was driven out by East River. My finds brought new light on the subject, although they were made thirty miles or so from Manhattan. Another important feature was that I was able to get two carbon-14 dates done on charcoal from a fire beneath the midden, and shells from the top of the midden. The dates showed that the site had been occupied between A.D. 1200 and 1250—they were the first dates for a coastal site!

In my studies, I looked at upper New York State archaeological information. The more I read, the more I became convinced that the East River pottery was just the result of trading and passing ideas along, down the Hudson from the north. The makers of East River pottery were the descendants of the Windsor potters. After all, the Hudson River must have been a great trade route, and Smith himself had shown that the prehistoric New Yorkers had been using arrow and spearpoints, stone axes, bannerstones, and pottery like the upstate people from the earliest periods. Further, the date of my early East River site in Connecticut fitted in with dates obtained in upper New York for the Owasco culture, with pottery so much like East River. Finally, the New Jersey site that Smith felt represented the home of East River was on the Delaware River, which

106

drained the New York area; therefore the people who lived there should have been getting trade goods and ideas from central New York State just the same as the prehistoric New Yorkers. If the New Jersey and East River sites had pottery that looked alike, couldn't one assume that they looked alike because they both had been influenced by the same group of Indians in upstate New York?

Smith and I exchanged ideas in print; other archaeologists took up the argument, too. This sort of thing happens in archaeology all the time. If only two people are working in an area, they will generally disagree on one important thing *at least*.

Since 1955, a lot more information has come up that puts our whole discussion in a new light and supports *all sides* of the argument in one way or another. First, there is evidence that prehistoric New York was in some kind of contact with the New Jersey Indians. Undeniable New Jersey pottery has been found on Staten Island, in Pelham Bay Park, and on Throgs Neck in the Bronx. The strange burial cult on eastern Long Island at the end of the Archaic period and various Archaic spearpoints found around New York City may also be the result of influence from west of the Hudson.

But we also know that the Hudson was carrying many things out of upper New York State to the sea shore. Pottery from the north was found on Staten Island by Jacobson, and Ritchie's research in the Hudson Valley has linked the whole of upstate New York with the coast from Archaic times up to the time that East River arose. Unfortunately, there is a gap in the record in the Hudson Valley during East River times but only a few good sites have been excavated and reported on so far (eight to be exact) and so there is a good chance that other sites will be found, excavated, and reported on, and the gap will be filled in some day.

In historic times, we know that the fierce Iroquois tribes held the Manhattan people in tribute and so we can assume that Iroquois war parties must have been traversing the river long before Verrazano, making another point of contact with the north.

Then there is the evidence we talked about in previous chapters: Archaic influence from the south and north and the Adena and Hopewell mound builders from Ohio in the early and middle Woodland period. All in all, the situation looks much more complicated than anyone imagined it to be ten years ago. But are we any closer to an answer to the original question: where did the East River pottery and its makers come from? Perhaps, perhaps not. We can see that there were many opportunities for the prehistoric New Yorkers to have picked up ideas from almost anywhere in the Northeast during most of prehistory. There is still no evidence of an East River "invasion." We have found no village sites that could be identified as definitely being from the Delaware River with Delaware River tools and Delaware-type skeletons. To *prove* a migration you must find such a village or villages. Without proof you can still hold an opinion or theory, however, and Smith's theory is still as good as it ever was, as is mine.

I suspect that after ten or twenty years we will find that Smith and I were both right in some ways, both wrong in other ways. This is the way things usually work out. For the time being, let us say that the mystery of the origin of East River pottery is still unsolved and will be until more clues are unearthed from the midden heaps and pits around Manhattan.

Aside from the pottery, the rest of the tools left behind by the East River people are not very much different from the earlier periods. Hunters and woodsmen still used the grooved axes and celts in their work and probably in war as well. The same kinds of hammerstones and antler flakers were used for making projectile points, scrapers, and knives. Arrowpoints changed markedly in shape: the characteristic East River variety is small and triangular, without a stem. The bones of the kills made with these arrows litter the midden heaps and provided raw material for bone tools of many kinds. The bones of animals were often shot back at their animal relatives in the form of bone arrowheads. Bone awls were used for

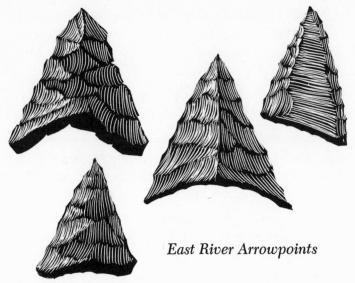

East River Arrowpoints

clothing and woodworking. One-hole bone needles, also possibly for clothing, have been found.

Agriculture still was important: more so, in all likelihood, than in early Woodland times. Corn was prepared using the same kinds of stone pestles and mortars used in earlier times. Harvests saw storage bins full of corn and beans all over Indian villages. Some of the pits used for garbage disposal by the East River Indians may have been originally storage pits. In other parts of the East, storage pits usually had sapling fences around them and a cover on top. They looked like small silos. After being used for storage for a time such pits were turned into refuse pits.

Bone fishhooks flashed in the water around Manhattan, luring fish to destruction in the bottom of large East River cooking pots, where corn, beans, shellfish, or meat simmered quietly. Netting was not forgotten, however, as the stone net-weights found on East River sites so clearly indicate.

During the East River period, the first really good evidence appears for the making of wampum. In the Baker Hill site, just outside the Queens County limits, a wampum factory of sorts must have existed. The shells of the periwinkle were gathered from the shores. The animals were removed (and probably found their way into the Indian pot). Then the outer spirals of the shell were broken away to reveal the

thick central column of the shell, around which the animal spiraled, building its succession of ever-larger seasonal houses. This thick column was cut into smaller sections with stone flake knives or saws, to make a series of fat barrel-shaped shell beads, which were then drilled from end to end for stringing.

When the Dutch had arrived, much later, bringing iron and steel trade tools with them, the Indians acquired small metal drills. This enabled them to make the much finer beads which are the "wampum" we know of today. Between 1936 and 1948, Dr. Solecki excavated an Indian fort at Corchaug on eastern Long Island which was used by the Indians after the Europeans had arrived. In the refuse deposits around Corchaug he found many fragments of the small beads in all stages of manufacture.

The dead of the East River people were buried like the early Windsor people. Most of the burials were "flexed": buried with knees drawn up to chest, as in the case described at the beginning of this chapter. "Secondary" burials, in which the body is first allowed to decay and then the bones cleaned, bundled up, and reburied, are also reported. These differences in forms of burial might be related to differences in the importance of the dead, or to the way they died. Unfortunately we know very little about this.

Human skeletons are not the only things found in

East River graves, however. Numerous Indian dog burials have also been found around New York City, and at least some of them have been found in graves of the East River period. The late Mr. Julius Lopez, a well known and dedicated amateur archaeologist in the New York area, reported on a dog burial which he and a companion, Mr. Stanley Wisniewski, excavated on College Point, across from La Guardia Airport. The dog was buried in the bottom of a shallow, dish-shaped pit, about three and a half feet wide and less than one foot deep. Within the pit were a series of strata, or layers. At the top was a layer of reddish soil mixed with shell ash, next a layer of grayish shell ash, then a layer of charcoal, followed by a layer of black soil. Below this, on the sandy subsoil, lay the

113

skeleton of a small dog, lacking both skull and tail. Near the dog skeleton were the crushed bones of a small, weasel-like animal called a "fisher," and some fragments of the dog skull, which appeared to have been burned or cooked. Some East River pottery fragments, a net sinker, a hammerstone, and a rubbing stone were also found in the pit. Four large stones were arranged around the pit as though for markers. Above the grave, a fire had been kindled. As Lopez pointed out, all the unusual details of the burial indicated that it was probably done as part of a ceremony in which the killing of the dog, possibly as some kind of sacrifice, was an important part. Other dog burials have been found at Bowman's Brook and Tottenville on Staten Island, at Throgs Neck, and at Pelham Bay in the Bronx. The only clue we have to hint at the fate of the Indian dogs in these burials is in the reports of the White Dog Ceremony of the Iroquois of upper New York State, in which dogs were burned alive. There is obviously still much to be learned about the prehistoric New Yorkers and their lives.

The only way that this can be learned is by further careful excavation in archaeological sites in the New York area. There is no magic way to find an archaeological site, nor does one have to depend on luck alone to search it out. Archaeologists simply look with patience in places where they know that

Indians lived and where sites have been found before: along the shores of bays and inlets, in rock shelters and caves, or along streams or rivers inland. When searching these areas, archaeologists keep a close eye on the ground, looking for shell fragments from a midden beneath the surface, chips of quartz or flint that might have been discarded by Indian arrow-point makers, and recognizable artifacts such as pottery or stone tools. Often, scattered shells only indicate the site of a clambake of ten years ago, but occasionally one hits the mark and finds a real site. When an area looks promising, archaeologists will often dig small test pits to check the subsurface conditions, see if midden material is, in fact, there, and get some idea of the extent of it, both in area and depth.

In Dr. Smith's study of coastal New York archaeology, a large table lists all the kinds of stone, bone, and shell tools known from the East River sites and the characteristics of the sites themselves. Reading past the shell beads, the pottery pipes, and potsherds found on the site one comes to another category at the very end of the table. This category is titled: "European trade goods." It contains some very un-Indian kinds of things, including bottle fragments, white clay pipes, gunflints, Jew's harps, and copper and brass tubes and sheets. These artifacts came from the site of an Indian fort at Massapequa, Long

115

Island, excavated in 1938 by the Flushing Historical Society. They were mixed in with potsherds of East River types: Eastern Incised and Bowman's Brook Incised. This mixture of artifacts, from the ruins of the crude fort of the Massapeags, marks the beginning of the end of Indian culture in the New York metropolitan area, as far as the archaeological record is concerned. It shows us that the Indians who met the colonists there were, in fact, the East River people whose origin has been disputed. It also tells us that the prehistoric record is exhausted: we must turn now to the pages of history to read the last chapter of the story of these vanished native New Yorkers.

There is a great difference between the point of view taken by an archaeologist and that by a traveler, seafarer, or historian describing living people. The archaeologist concentrates on very small details of imperishable tools and utensils. The traveler or historian, however, tends to see life as a more well-knit whole and pays little attention to the details of tools, etc. They are more interested in describing the people, their behavior and personalities, their ceremonies, and the more "human" side of life in general. And so in changing from the prehistoric to the historic viewpoint, we, too, will have some gear-changing to do, as we see, through the eyes of the Dutch settlers, the East River people gradually surrendering their lands and their lives to the foreign invaders.

5 · Long Shadows of the Trail's End

THE BOAT RODE LOW in the calm waters of the harbor, crammed with the new settlers, their belongings, and the supplies necessary to keep them alive until their farming and gardening would permit them to be self-sufficient. The voyage had been long, made worse by cramped quarters on the overcrowded vessel. But these people who were coming ashore in the long boats that shuttled back and forth between ship and shore were not used to many of the comforts of life.

Their strangely accented Dutch marked them as Walloons, French speakers from the lowlands of what is now Belgium, and they were accustomed to persecution, wars, and endless troubles in the land from which they had come. They were not intellectuals—far from it. Like most European peasants of the time, they were nearly all illiterate. These were tough, wild farmers, who knew how to scrape a living from poor soil. They were coming in hopes of finding a better life in New Netherland than in their

homeland, but they were not particularly interested in ideals of freedom.

Their clothing was rough and meant to stand long wear. Many went barefoot and were quite at home doing so. Men and women alike had been stamped with the marks of hard physical labor: weather-beaten, wrinkled faces, gnarled hands covered with calluses and scars, and the sagging posture of those whose lot it is to work in the fields, dawn to dusk, for their whole useful lives.

Age came quickly to such people, and life was to be enjoyed whenever possible, lest the opportunity never return. These were people who could work hard all week and drink and carouse just as hard on a Saturday night. Fights and escapades of all sorts were a good source of entertainment. But they were ideally suited for survival in this new land, because it was not a place for weaklings or "summer soldiers." Only the strong would survive the Indians, animals, hunger, disease, and the weather, not to mention the two months on a tiny ship, pitching and wallowing through the great swells of the grim Atlantic.

The new arrivals did not remain long together on Manhattan Island. Only a few of the thirty families stayed there as settlers. The rest moved out soon, some on boats, some on foot, to the far ends of the colony. One group journeyed northeastward into the Connecticut area. Another moved across the East

River into Long Island, and another headed down into Delaware country, across the Hudson. And they were but the first of many to come.

The arrival of this group of settlers in 1623, under the leadership of Cornelius Jacobsen May, marked another turning point in the history of New York and its Indian inhabitants. Until this time, the Dutch interest in New York had been solely commercial. Dutch merchants had formed a company for trade with the New Netherland after the return of Hudson, and ships picked up large quantities of furs and skins of all types for the clothing of wealthy Europeans. But the arrival of the Walloons marked the beginning of settlement. The island of Manhattan was no longer to be just a trading post, it was to be the site of a town in a colony soon to be dotted with little towns and farms. The Indians could not hope to stand against this invasion.

When the prehistoric New Yorkers emerge onto the pages of history, they are organized into three major tribal groups. The Manhattan tribe, occupying the present island itself and some adjacent area, belonged to a tribal union known as the Wappinger Confederacy. Eight tribes belonged to the confederacy, which extended from Manhattan Island up the Hudson some fifty miles and up the coast to the Housatonic River in Connecticut. The Wappinger tribes were: the Wappinger, Manhattan, Kitchawank, Tankiteke, Nochpeem, Siwanoy, Sintsink, and Wecquaesgeeck. Across the Hudson from the Wappinger lands was the territory of the Lenape (Delaware) Indians, who held Staten Island. The Long Island tribes were known as the Metoac. Thirteen different tribal groups are known to have existed on Long Island, but it is only the western Metoac tribes that are of interest to us. These include many tribes whose names (today sometimes differently spelled) are very familiar to New Yorkers as place names: Canarsee, the Massapequa, Merric, Matinecock, Nesaquake, and Rockaway.

The boundaries of the tribal lands are no longer known, so a very exact map of territories can't be drawn. Throughout these tribal lands were scattered villages and hamlets, usually in good defensive positions and near water sources. Shoreline sites were popular around New Netherland. Some of the villages were simply clusters of the familiar bark-covered or thatched houses, round or oval in plan. Some had rounded roofs, others are reported by the Dutch to have had flat roofs.

Some villages were surrounded by fortifications consisting of low mounds on which wooden log fences, or palisades, were built. One Dutch observer saw a curious but apparently effective way of building timber palisades: logs were piled on the ground, on each side of these, other logs were set into the earth at angles so that they would cross like an "X"

122

above the piled logs. These upright logs were lashed at the point where they crossed, and additional logs were piled in the upper angle of the "X." Not all villages were fortified, however. Some may have had a fort standing nearby to which the inhabitants could flee in case of war.

In some places and at certain times of the year, the Indians of New Netherland did not live in villages, either. Many seem to have lived in little hamlets consisting of a single large house inhabited by a number of families or a few small houses grouped together.

Two of the early Dutch visitors to New York, Jaspar Dankers and Peter Sluyter, visited a hamlet of the Nyack, a branch of the Canarsee, near what is now Fort Hamilton. There they were shown a house about sixty feet long and fourteen feet wide that

sheltered about six to eight families in its arched interior. The house was open along the top from end to end to let out the smoke from the cooking fires within. Because of the narrowness of the house and its curving sides, it was possible to stand only in the center. Another Dutch visitor saw a single house one hundred feet long and twenty feet wide, housing sixteen to eighteen families. Dankers and Sluyter wrote that these large houses were inhabited by individuals who were all related to a common ancestor, such as a man, his wife, their married male children and their wives and children, and their unmarried daughters.

These houses may not have been inhabited all year round, for even at the arrival of the Europeans the native New Yorkers moved about a good bit during any given year. Hunting seasons might see the families in the woods on good hunting lands, while planting time would find them near their fields. At other times they might live in the larger villages.

The tribal organization of the Indians around New York City is not very clearly known. This was one topic that the Dutch must have known a lot about, but they just neglected to pass it on to us. The old land grants seem to show that the tribes were made up of a number of smaller groups or sub-tribes, each occupying some area within the tribal territory. Each of these sub-tribes was in turn made up of numerous large family groups of the type described above that

124

generally tended to live and work together throughout most of the year. There was probably some kind of clan organization, by which a number of families throughout the whole tribe claimed to be descended from a mythical animal from the legendary past—a "totem" animal, or ancestor-god. Property and power was passed from father to son and the tribal chief was a male. The chief had considerable power over his tribesmen: he could decree death as a punishment for certain crimes although he usually did not concern himself with stealing and "small" crimes. A tribal council existed, apparently made up of senior men of the sub-tribes or the families within the sub-tribes. The chiefs consulted with these advisors on most decisions of importance.

The tribes of New York were not completely free to do as they pleased. They, like many other tribes of the whole Northeast, lived in mortal fear of the Iroquois, whose war parties spread death and destruction wherever they went. The Iroquois were ferocious fighters. The most horrible crimes were but entertainment to these grim bandits of the woods. Nothing delighted them more than to bring back a prisoner alive, for then the Iroquois womenfolk could enjoy one of their specialties—torture in its cruelest form.

Inside the simple houses of the Indians of New York life too was rather simple. Fires were ranged up and down the center line of the long houses for each family's cooking needs and for warmth. The inhabitants slept on mats spread along the outside walls, their feet toward the fire. Like many other peoples of the world, the Indians were accustomed to squat, rather than sit on the ground or on a raised object. This position is very tiring to people like us who are not used to it. It is quite restful to many folk from other parts of the world, such as the Japanese, the Polynesians, and the Koreans, who can squat for hours.

Scattered about the floors of these houses and hung from the walls were the utensils and tools necessary for life: pottery vessels, baskets, wooden bowls and spoons, weapons, fishing nets and line, sometimes canoes and paddles, extra clothing, and food supplies. None of the items made of wood or fiber have survived in the damp earth of the New York metropolitan area. It is clear from the description of the archaeological finds, and the description of what the Dutchmen *saw*, that archaeologists really have only a very small amount of information to go on when they begin to reconstruct a dead way of life such as that of the prehistoric New Yorkers.

Life within the Indian houses seemed very casual to the Dutch visitors who have left their experiences for us to share. There do not seem to have been any fixed meal times, for we are told that each individual ate alone, whenever he felt like it, regardless of what the rest of his family or the other families in the hut were doing.

The most important foods were, of course, corn and beans, harvested from gardens that were cleared from forest land by groups of relatives and neighbors working together. The men did most of the heavy work in the clearing of the land. Then the women tended the gardens, while the men devoted themselves to work befitting men: fishing and hunting. Nets of many varieties as well as hooks and lines served to land good catches of fish. Shellfish were collected in spring and fall and dried for use later. The younger men, eager to be off on the hunt, sometimes left their fishing chores early in the fall, but the older more experienced men waited until winter had

127

really arrived. Winter hunting seems to have been done with traps and snares, ranging in size from small ones for beavers, etc. to those large enough to take a deer, the Indians' favorite source of meat (if the number of deer bones in Indian middens is any indication).

Indian fare was not elaborate and would probably seem heavy and rather tasteless to us. Corn meal, ground between stone mortars and pestles, was prepared in a number of ways. The most popular form was cornmeal "mush," like some of our modern hot breakfast foods. Into this mush, just about any other kind of food available would be thrown. Fish, meat, shellfish, nuts, berries, beans, and squash, as well as many other things, all found their way into the pot in a kind of catch-all stew which must have been quite nourishing but certainly not very attractive to see. Cornmeal mixed with water was also baked into cakes in the ashes of the fire, as was nut meat, made of acorns, for example. Cornmeal was also carried and eaten dry on trips as a kind of "emergency ration."

The native New Yorker of the seventeenth century was very much like his prehistoric ancestors in appearance. The Indian skeletons from around New York City have not been studied very extensively, but they seem to share certain general features. These Indians had long, narrow heads, with wide

cheekbones and heavy jaws. Their teeth showed
much evidence of wear from chewing coarse meats
and vegetables and from the abrasive action of the
small bits of stones that were constantly breaking
from the grindstones and pestles and getting mixed
into the cornmeal. By comparison with the European
sailors, soldiers, and settlers who were streaming into
New Amsterdam, the native New Yorkers were tall,
and well built. Their skins were of a brownish or
bronze color and their hair straight and black. The
women wore their hair in long braids on either side
of their heads, while the men wore theirs in various
different ways. Some shaved both sides of their head,
leaving a long strip down the center. Others shaved
one side and left the other long. Men and women
both shaved their heads in mourning. They were not
the cleanest people, as their way of life did not really
permit them to be. During winter, bathing was impossible. During the summer, in order to have some
protection from the clouds of insects hovering
around the swamps and bogs of Long Island, Manhattan, and Staten Island, they covered their skins
with oils and greases which did not always have the
most pleasant odor. Sweat baths were a favorite
method of bathing as well as a "cure" for many
diseases.

The wardrobe of the Indians of New York was simple. The men wore breech cloths of skin or fabric, and

the women short skirts, both held up with belts of snakeskin ornamented with shell beads. Fur robes were used in warm weather as well as in cold. In the winter, however, moccasins and leggings were usually added to the men's clothing, and heavier robes and upper garments put on. It is possible that some fitted jackets or trousers were also used, but the Dutch do not mention this kind of clothing. The leggings were made of skin, covering the legs from moccasin top to hip. Moccasins to keep out the bite of frost and snow were of deerskin and sometimes of corn husks. Shell ornaments were worn on ears, necks, and wrists. Faces of both men and women were painted with black stripes. Men used other colors as well. Feathers of the many birds which inhabited the Manhattan area were worked into hair and clothing for decoration. Elaborate fur headdresses were sometimes worn. While adults wore relatively little clothing, children wore less. Boys went naked until the age of twelve, while little girls simply wore small aprons from infancy on.

The streets of New York today echo to the sounds of many languages from all points of the globe. Chinese, Korean, Tibetan, Armenian, Arabic, Bantu, Swahili, and many others can be heard, if only one knows the place to go. But the language of our prehistoric New Yorkers—Algonkian—is heard no more: it exists only in the pages of books wherein some

4

thoughtful missionary, soldier, or traveler long ago took the time to jot down a few words for things or some simple phrases. In the early twentieth century M. R. Harrington, one of America's great Indian archaeologists and ethnologists, visited a settlement of the Shinnecock Indians on eastern Long Island. He found that a few older people recalled some Indian words but that no one could speak the language any more. Harrington recorded these words and published them with words from other Algonkian-speaking tribes in New England and New Jersey. They will give some idea of what the Indian language spoken in prehistoric New York sounded like.

English	—	Shinnecock
turtle	—	matci′k
snake	—	skuk
man	—	tcais
woman	—	wi′nai, skwa
child	—	papu′s
sea-beach	—	siwaa′
rain	—	ke′mio
house	—	wi′kam
corn mush	—	suppa′n
shellfish	—	se′tcawa
thanks!	—	tabutni′
greetings!	—	hah′cami
come quick!	—	mekwi′

Never make the mistake of thinking that this language was somehow childish or simple, just because it was spoken by a people who were living a primitive kind of existence. The Algonkian languages are complicated, with a grammar that is much more elaborate than English. The Indians had to provide for all the necessities of life for themselves and to do so effectively, their language couldn't be simple or childlike. Anthropologists and linguists who have studied the languages of the primitive peoples of the world have found that *all* of them are fully as good as our own for expressing complicated ideas. In some cases, European languages can express some ideas better, in certain other cases, Indian languages can do so more clearly. Missionaries who traveled and lived among the Algonkian and Iroquois tribes of what is now New York State and Canada in the seventeenth century marveled at how well suited the Indian languages were to arguing about complicated matters of religion with their Indian hosts.

The Dutch were good staunch Christians and seem to have regarded the Indian religion as devil worship, pure and simple. Adriaan Van der Donck, a Dutchman who visited New Netherland in 1656, describes the ceremonies that he witnessed:

They begin with jumping, crying, and grinning, as if they were possessed and mad. They kindle large fires, and dance around and over the same, lengthwise and across; they roll, tumble overhead, and bend themselves, and continue their violent exercises until the sweat pours out and streams down to their feet. . . . During these operations, all their devil-drivers join in the rolling and howling, when they altogether appear to be crazy. When their charming has continued some time, then the devil, as they say, appears to them in the form of a beast. If the beast be a ravenous animal, it is a bad omen; if it be a harmless creature, the sign is better; the animal gives them strange answers to their inquiries, but seldom so clear and distinct that they can comprehend or interpret the same, which, however, they strike at as a blind man does at an egg. If they interpret the answers incorrectly, the fault is theirs,—sometimes they utter things beyond the devil's texts.

What Van der Donck witnessed was, of course, not the worship of the Christian devil, but the calling up of an animal spirit, perhaps one of the totem animals, to serve as an oracle. The religion of all the Algonkian groups involved large numbers cf animal spirits, dwarfs of the forests, ghosts, and monsters of various kinds. Some students of Indian lore believe that there was also a belief in a god who ruled above all the other gods. Van der Donck questioned a New York Indian about this. The Indian scornfully told him that such a god did indeed exist, but that he was so busy wooing a beautiful goddess that he had forgotten about his creations, where the evil spirits were running wild in his absence.

134

Village ceremonies were held at harvest time and in times of war or preparation for it. Offerings of wampum were placed in dishes upon the house roofs and an Indian magician—a "pawaw"—called upon the gods to take them. Sooner or later a bird, an animal, or a human would appear, and the audience would accept the animal or human as a representation of the spirit.

The pawaw who officiated at these ceremonies was also a magical healer who could cure by reciting or chanting spells over an ill person. Nevertheless, death came to all sooner or later, and the New Yorkers believed that there was a life after death. They buried their dead with clothings and belongings, fencing the grave to protect it from wild animals as described in the previous chapter. Mourning was not easy: the relatives of the dead shaved their heads, painted their faces black, and visited the grave daily until the paint wore off. The names of the dead were not mentioned, even if they involved a word used in everyday speech. A new word was made up to fill the gap!

The Iroquois may have been the "wolves" of the northeastern Woodlands, but it would be wrong to think of the prehistoric New Yorkers as gentle and peace-loving people. War was a part of Woodland life; not war as we know it, with huge armies sprawling across miles of territory, but the dirty, brutal war of raid, ambush, torture, and murder that is so common among many primitive tribes. The forts around Indian villages in the New York area were not only to protect against the Iroquois, they were also a protection against other tribes in the immediate area.

The weapons of hunting—bows, arrows, knives, spears, axes—were also the weapons of war. Square shields were carried by the New York Indians for protection from the feathered shafts of the enemy. Most of the destruction and killing seems to have taken place in raids and ambushes, where the attacker had the advantage of surprise and made good use of it. In open fighting, face to face, the eastern Indians were much less courageous, however. When facing a foe across an open field, "war" became more of a game of dodging arrows and spears while trying to shoot your own arrows. Beheading or scalping war casualties for "trophies" was common. Slow, terrible torture was all that a prisoner could expect. Some were cut up, piece by piece, while still alive, others scalped and burned with live coals, still others were pulled apart by ropes attached to arms and legs, while some were left tied to stakes in the swamps to die from insect and animal bites and starvation.

In such societies, strangers are never welcome, particularly if the strangers are completely different from anyone seen before. A stranger is an unknown quantity, almost certainly a threat. This is why Hudson's sounding party was attacked so soon after the *Half Moon* crew had held "open-house" for their Indian hosts. A few weeks later, further up the river, the Indians visiting the *Half Moon* began to steal whatever they could carry off. One was shot, another had his arm hacked off by Dutch steel when he attempted to overturn a *Half Moon* long-boat. A fleet of canoes attacked the little vessel but were driven off by a volley of musketry and a cannon shot. If *visitors* were on such uncertain ground, it doesn't take much imagination to see what the Indians thought when they realized that permanent settlers were moving in on their lands. Even though these lands had been paid for, as in the famous sale of Manhattan for twenty-four dollars worth of trinkets and coats, the Indians' world was being tightened

around them. Fences were up, boundaries were very clear, and the Dutch had different ideas about property from the Indians, who were much freer with gifts and help to each other.

Add to the warrior temperament of the Indians the stubborn and equally warlike ways of the tough Dutch settlers, traders, and military people who were arriving at New Amsterdam, and you have an explosive mixture. Trouble was caused by both sides in a succession of incidents, some big, some small. In 1626 the servants of Peter Minuit, the director-general of the colony, robbed and killed an Indian of the Wecquaesgeeck tribe who was visiting the little town. A younger Indian boy accompanying the victim fled to the woods again, vowing to bring revenge at some later time. Minuit, always mindful of the Indian threat, imported a military engineer to design and build a fort for the little colony, but work went slowly, even though there was constant news of friction between Indians and whites.

Minuit's successor, a man named Van Twiller, imported 104 soldiers to man the fortifications, such as they were at that time. The Dutch soldiers must have presented an awesome sight to the Indians around the colony. They wore shiny body armor and helmets, and were equipped with swords, daggers, wheellock and snaphance muskets, and cannon. They were also disciplined to open field fighting against fierce European foes such as the Spanish and Portuguese. It was not long, however, before the Indians themselves got guns and ammunition. They soon became very good marksmen and then the Dutch were no longer safe inside their armor.

Van Twiller was sent home for misconduct in 1638 and replaced by Director-General Kieft, whose main talent seems to have been causing trouble. A pig was stolen on Staten Island, so Kieft sent seventy soldiers to raid the Indian settlements there. For such a small crime, many Indians were killed and the Indian crops destroyed, and the grievances the Indians already had against the Europeans increased. This attack brought swift retaliation by the Indians: they

swooped down on the little settlements around the Bronx, Long Island, and Manhattan, killing, stealing, and burning. The Indian boy whose uncle had been killed by Minuit's servant in 1626 returned to keep his vow of vengeance. He killed an unsuspecting Dutch wheelwright, Claes Smits, at the outset of the reign of terror. The bitter war of sneak attacks went on for weeks and months. It soon became clear that neither Indians nor Europeans would have any crops —the war kept men too busy to plant.

Kieft sent a Captain De Vries, an intelligent artillery officer, to try to arrange a peace. At a conference with the Indians near Rockaway, De Vries listened while the Indians recounted the evil deeds of the Europeans, placing a stick on the ground as a marker for each grievance. After much patient talk and promises the brave De Vries got some of the chiefs to come to the fort. He was sure that Kieft would give them a royal welcome. Much to his surprise, Kieft gave such poor gifts to his guests that all De Vries's work was undone! The chiefs departed angry and the war continued!

Kieft was finally recalled to Europe, and was replaced by the famous Peter Stuyvesant, a man who believed in the use of force. Nevertheless, Stuyvesant did not impress the Indians too much. He did not treat his own countrymen well, either, and angered many of them by his arrogant manner at a

140

conference held to make defense plans against Indian raids in 1654.

When an old Indian woman was shot and killed while picking peaches in the orchard of farmer Van Dyck, the war paint was made ready, bows were restrung, and arrows fletched. While Stuyvesant was on a journey to the Delaware River area in 1655, the Indians attacked New Amsterdam itself with a fleet of sixty-four canoes, killing and looting. After their task there was finished, they struck out for Hoboken and Staten Island. When the dust of battle had settled the Dutch counted 100 of their number killed and 152 taken prisoner. Stuyvesant returned and set about stopping the rebellion. He seems to have done well at calming the Indians, for when the fighting stopped, there was peace for three years.

Nevertheless, there was still trouble further up the Hudson where whites and Indians were murdering each other regularly. In 1663 Indian war started again with another massacre. By this time neither the Dutch East India Company nor the colonists gave Stuyvesant much support, and he was in deep trouble. By 1664, however, his troubles were over, for a British fleet entered the bay and occupied the city. Dutch rule (and Stuyvesant's responsibility!) was ended forever.

Under English rule, the Indians found they had a new enemy to cope with: disease. Epidemics of Eu-

ropean diseases, to which the Indians had no im-
munity, began to carry off many of the native New
Yorkers. An English writer in 1670, only sixty-one
years after Hudson's arrival, remarked that there
were very few Indians left in the Manhattan area. As
the years passed this small number dwindled even
further, through war, disease, and poverty. Others
married settlers or slaves, and their children grew up
as whites or Negroes, but not as Indians. Within two
centuries of Hudson's arrival, New York no longer
had any "Indian problem" and soon all the native
New Yorkers had shuffled off in their moccasined feet
down the path of ghosts. Their land was gone and so
were they. Ten thousand years or more of prehistory
were ended in a few short decades, ten thousand
years for which no records exist except lonely un-
marked graves; crude tools of stone, bone, and shell
scattered around shell middens; and the cold ashes
and charcoal of long-dead campfires.

From these meager remains, archaeologists have
managed to gain a glimpse of what life was like in
those days. We can now talk easily of spans of years
that are too big for our small imaginations really to
understand. But there is more waiting in the earth
around New York—more pages of the missing chapters of New York prehistory to be uncovered and
fitted into their proper places. As each year goes by,
more buildings rise into the sky, more highways sear

their way across the face of the city and its environs, and more of these archaeological sites are destroyed. It is a race against time. Who will win: the archaeologist or the bulldozer?

Bibliography

Those who are interested in doing further reading about the archaeology of New York City should read the original reports and papers upon which this book is based.

The most important report, summarizing all archaeological research in the New York area up to 1949, is:

Smith, C. S. "The Archaeology of Coastal New York," *Anthropological Papers of the American Museum of Natural History*, Vol. 43, Part 2, New York, 1950. This volume contains a complete bibliography of all published reports and historical documents up to 1949.

Since 1949, a number of additional studies have appeared. These deal with the archaeology and the ancient climate of the New York region. Reports of archaeological investigations in other areas related to New York have also been published. The most important of these, used in this book, are given below:

Bloom, A. L., and Stuiver, M. "Submergence of the Connecticut Coast," *Science*, Vol. 139, No. 3552, Washington, D.C., 25 January 1963.

145

Bibliography

Boyd, Glenda F. "The Transitional Phase on Long Island," *American Antiquity*, Vol. 27, No. 4, Salt Lake City, April 1962.

Brennan, L. A. "A 6,000-Year-Old Shell Midden on the Hudson River," *Eastern States Archeological Federation Bulletin*, No. 23, Trenton, June 1964.

Byers, D. S. "An Introduction to Five Papers on the Archaic Stage," *American Antiquity*, Vol. 24, No. 3, Salt Lake City, January 1959.

———. "The Eastern Archaic: Some Problems and Hypotheses," *American Antiquity*, Vol. 24, No. 3, Salt Lake City, January 1959.

Byers, D. S., and Rouse, I. "A Re-examination of the Guida Farm," *Bulletin of the Archeological Society of Connecticut*, No. 30, New Haven, October 1960.

Carter, G. F. "Sea-Level-Time and Coastal Archeology in the East," *Eastern States Archeological Federation Bulletin*, No. 17, Trenton, January 1958.

Donn, W. L., and Shaw, D. M. "Sea Level and Climate of the Past Century," *Science*, Vol. 142, No. 3596, Washington, D.C., 29 November 1963.

Harrington, M. R. "An Ancient Village Site of the Shinnecock Indians," *Anthropological Papers of the American Museum of Natural History*, Vol. 22, Part 5, New York, 1924.

Hester, J. J. "Late Pleistocene Extinction and Radiocarbon Dating," *American Antiquity*, Vol. 26, No. 1, Salt Lake City, July 1960.

Jacobson, J. "History and Prehistory at Tottenville, New York," *Eastern States Archeological Federation Bulletin*, No. 21, Trenton, March 1962.

Lopez, J. "Preliminary Report on the Schurz Site, Throgs

Bibliography

Neck, the Bronx," *Bulletin of the Nassau Archeological Society*, Bulletin No. 1, Sea Cliff, N.Y., Summer 1955.
——. "The Pelham Boulder Site, Bronx County, New York," *Eastern States Archeological Federation Bulletin*, No. 15, Trenton, January 1956.
——. "A Birdstone Fragment from New York City," *American Antiquity*, Vol. 22, No. 4, Salt Lake City, April 1957.
——. "Curvilinear Design Elements in the New York Coastal Area," *Bulletin of the Archeological Society of Connecticut*, No. 28, New Haven, February 1958.
——. "Curvilinear Motifs on New York Coastal Pottery: A Reply," *American Antiquity*, Vol. 24, No. 4, Salt Lake City, April 1959.
Lopez, J., and Wisniewski, S. "Discovery of a Possible Ceremonial Dog Burial in the City of Greater New York," *Bulletin of the Archeological Society of Connecticut*, No. 29, New Haven, December 1958.
McKusick, M. "The Pottery of the NAS II Site, Long Island," *Eastern States Archeological Federation Bulletin*, No. 15, Trenton, January 1956.
Patterson, E. D. "Garvie Point—NAS Site I," *Bulletin of the Nassau Archeological Society*, No. 1, Sea Cliff, N.Y., Summer 1955.
Peets, O. H. "Experiments in the Use of Atlatl Weights," *American Antiquity*, Vol. 26, No. 1, Salt Lake City, July 1960.
Rainey, F. G. "A Compilation of Historical Data Contributing to the Ethnography of Connecticut and Southern New England Indians," *Bulletin of the Archeological Society of Connecticut*, Reprint No. 3, New Haven, March 1956.

Bibliography

Ritchie, W. A. "An Introduction to Hudson Valley Pre-history," *New York State Museum and Science Service,* Bulletin No. 367, Albany, January 1958.

———. "The Development of Aboriginal Settlement Patterns in the Northeast: A Progress Report," *Eastern States Archeological Federation Bulletin,* No. 17, Trenton, January 1958.

———. "The Stony Brook Site and Its Relation to Archaic and Transitional Cultures on Long Island," *New York State Museum and Science Service,* Bulletin No. 372, Albany, 1959.

———. "The Antiquity of Pottery in the Northeast," *American Antiquity,* Vol. 27, No. 4, Salt Lake City, April 1962.

Ritchie, W. A., Lenig, D., and Miller, P. S. "An Early Owasco Sequence in New York." *New York State Museum and Science Service,* Circular 32, Albany, October 1953.

Robbins, Maurice. "Wapanucket No. 6: An Archaic Village in Middleboro, Massachusetts," *Massachusetts Archeological Society,* Cohannet Chapter, 1959.

Robbins, M., and Agogino, G. A. "The Wapanucket No. 8 Site: A Clovis-Archaic Site in Massachusetts," *American Antiquity,* Vol. 29, No. 4, Salt Lake City, April 1964.

Salwen, B. "Sea Levels and Archeology in the Long Island Sound Area," *American Antiquity,* Vol. 28, No. 1, Salt Lake City, July 1962.

Sears, P. B. "Vegetation, Climate, and Coastal Submergence in Connecticut," *Science,* Vol. 140, No. 3562, Washington, D.C., 5 April 1963.

Smith, C. S. "Revised Chronology for the Archeology of

Coastal New York," *Bulletin of the Nassau Archeological Society,* Bulletin No. 1, Sea Cliff, N.Y., Summer 1955.

——. "The East River and Windsor Aspects: A Reply," *American Antiquity,* Vol. 23, No. 2, Salt Lake City, October 1957.

Solecki, R. "The Archeological Position of Historic Fort Corchaug, L.I., and Its Relation to Contemporary Forts," *Bulletin of the Archeological Society of Connecticut,* No. 24, New Haven, June 1950.

Stuiver, M., and Daddario, J. J. "Submergence of the New Jersey Coast," *Science,* Vol. 142, No. 3594, Washington, D.C., 15 November 1963.

Suggs, R. C. "Coastal New York and Connecticut Prehistory Reinterpreted," *American Antiquity,* Vol. 22, No. 4, Salt Lake City, April 1957.

——. "Radiocarbon Dates from the Manakaway Site, Connecticut," *American Antiquity,* Vol. 23, No. 4, Salt Lake City, April 1958.

——. "The Manakaway Site, Greenwich, Connecticut," *Bulletin of the Archeological Society of Connecticut,* No. 29, New Haven, December 1958.

Waters, J. H. "Some Animals Used as Food by Successive Cultural Groups in New England," *Bulletin of the Archeological Society of Connecticut,* No. 31, New Haven, December 1962.

Wormington, H. M. "Ancient Man in North America," *Denver Museum of Natural History, Popular Series No. 4,* Fourth Edition, Denver, 1957.

Index

222

222

pottery (*cont.*)
  of East River Indians:
    "Bowman's Brook Incised," 99–100
    "Clason Point Stamped," 100
    "Eastern Incised," 100–107
    "East River tradition," 97–99
  of Woodland Indians:
    "Clearview Stamped," 86
    "North Beach Brushed," 86
    "Vinette I," 86
    "Windsor tradition," 84–86, 90, 97–98, 104, 105

religion (*see also* supernatural artifacts):
  of Archaic Indians, 50–51
  of East River Indians, 133–135
  of Woodland Indians, 75–76
Ritchie, William, Dr., 52–53, 77, 88, 108

seriation, 81–83
sewing, 47, 110
shellfishing (*see also* fishing), 40, 48, 72, 111, 127
Skinner, Alonson, Dr., 52, 77, 78, 88, 99
Sluyter, Peter, 123–124
Smith, Carlyle, Dr., 53, 77–80, 82–87, 97, 99, 103, 105, 106–107, 109, 115
Solecki, Ralph, Dr., 96, 99, 112
spearpoints, 22–24, 42–43, 55, 88
spearthrowers, 45–46 88
stone-boiling, 87
storage bins, 110
stratigraphy, 52, 79
Stuyvesant, Peter, 140–142
Suggs, Robert C., Dr., 105–106, 107, 109
supernatural artifacts, 51, 55, 135

tobacco (*see also* pipes), 68, 102

Index

tools:
  Archaic period, 44, 46, 47, 50, 55–56
  East River Indian, 99, 109
  Paleo-Indian, 23, 24, 26
  Woodland period, 71, 73
  Transitional period (of Archaic culture), 56

ulu, 47

Van der Donck, Adriaan, 133–134
Van Twiller, 138, 139
vegetation:
  of Archaic period, 40
  of Paleo-Indian period, 28
Verrazano, Giovanni da, 5, 108

wampum, 111–112, 135
Wappinger Confederacy, 121
warfare:
  of East River Indians with Dutch, 136–142
  of Iroquois, 135
  of Woodland Indians, 135–136
weapons (*see also* artifacts, hunting):
  of Dutch, 137, 138
  of Indians, 11, 22, 26, 72, 136
weaving, 74
weirs, 49
White Dog Ceremony, 114
Windsor tradition pottery, *see* pottery
Wisniewski, Stanley, 113
Woodland Indians, 65–98, 108, 135

ABOUT THE AUTHOR

Robert C. Suggs is both a practicing anthropologist and an archaeologist. His current work in anthropology centers on social and psychological problems in modern complex societies.

Dr. Suggs has conducted several archaeological investigations on sites in Connecticut, New York, and Maryland; he has led an expedition in the Marquesas Islands of French Polynesia; and he has engaged in anthropological research in Tahiti and Fiji. He has published numerous scientific papers and books on his work.

He was born in Port Chester, New York. He received his B.A., M.A., and Ph.D., in anthropology, from Columbia University. He now lives in Alexandria, Virginia.

ABOUT THE ILLUSTRATOR

Leonard Everett Fisher received his early training at the Art Students League, at the studio of Moses and Raphael Soyer, and at the Heckscher Foundation in New York City. He was graduated from the Yale University School of Fine Arts with both a B.F.A. and M.F.A. degree.

During World War II, Mr. Fisher served in the Army as a topographic editor and a photogrammetrist (making maps from photographs). He has been dean of the Whitney School of Art in New Haven, Connecticut, and now devotes his time to painting, and to designing and illustrating books.